**W9-CEJ-086**

# *The Ghost Of Alcatraz*

*by*
*John F. Dekker*

**Published by**
**PAGET FILMS**
**202 Hoyt Street**
**Buffalo, NY 14213**
**© Copyright 1993 by John F. Dekker**

*Printed by*
Delta Printing Solutions

*Dedicated to my wife, Linda E. Dekker*

She insisted that I had a story to tell and I should tell it. She labored at my side with a whip in her hand until I had finished it. She guided me through the rough waters when I wanted to call it quits; through my discouragement and self-doubt, she was my walking dictionary . . Because of her, this book is now in print. I ask you one more question, Honey. How do you spell, "THANKS?"

# Foreword

I'm convinced that when John Dekker decided to enter a life of crime a few dimestores and banks were bound to take some hits, but the biggest loss of all would be to the world of comedy.

He is a damn funny man. Not everyone agrees. Not everyone gets his deadpan humor. I think it's because they are afraid of him. Perhaps they should be.

Luckily he has written this rollicking autobiography, so we can all enjoy the wry wit of this world-class wiseacre from a safe distance, with our wallets and watches securely in place - save for a few dollars to cover the price of the book.

Dekker's life story is no joke. He grew up on Chicago's hardscrabble south side during the Great Depression, committed grievous crimes, attempted desperate escapes, and did hard time on Alcatraz, the most fearsome prison in America. How he ever made it to 80 years old, a free man in good spirits with a loyal wife and beautiful grandchildren, is a mystery that unravels in these pages. But I suspect that his keen sense of humor played an integral role in this story of survival and redemption. As Victor Borge said, "Humor is the truth." And the truth shall set you free.

I first met John Dekker while making a documentary film about the annual reunion of ex-convicts and guards at the legendary Alcatraz prison. Turns out Dekker was one of the few known surviving ex-inmates of Alcatraz, and lived just up the road from the old island penitentiary in Vacaville, California. I had the bad timing to arrive at his front door during the horse races. He invited me in but wouldn't even talk to me for about 20 minutes.

Eventually, Dekker fessed up he was inmate #1076 from Alcatraz, and after a good deal of ribbing and more than a few wisecracks, he agreed to be interviewed for the film. We set up the camera and lights in his living room, and talked for about an hour. He called me worse than the FBI interrogators. Finally, I posed the last question: "Have you ever met, in later years, one of the victims of your crimes?"

It was a question I had asked other ex-cons of Alcatraz and it usually evoked heartfelt sentiments and teary-eyed apologies. With a downcast face, Dekker seemed similarly remorseful. "No, never met any victims of my crimes. But if I did, I'd tell'em 'I'm sorry. I probably scared the hell out of ya, but I'm sorry,'" he said. A brief pause, pregnant with sincere regret; and then with impeccable timing he stared down the lens of the camera: "And then I'd pull a gun on 'em and take his money." He said it with a straight face – a face that, even at 76 years old, appeared menacing. But there was something, a slight twinkle in one eye that told me he was only kidding. Or was he?

*-John Paget, Documentary Filmmaker*
***"Alcatraz Reunion"***
*AlcatrazFilm.com*

September 10th, 2008
Buffalo, New York

## Acknowledgements

To my many friends who have faithfully promised to buy one of my books: Gary (Red) Starnes, who laughed at my jokes and stories about Alcatraz; to my gold-mining partner, Lee Greer, who said, "Write a book, you've got a gold mine at your fingertips; and to my old boss, Ron Wilkes, who trusted me with the keys to his store and the combination to his safe. I needed that . . .

Special thanks to Dolores Krause; this seventy-year-old lady can really make a computer dance.

And last, but not least: the Golden Gate National Recreation Area and the staff on Alcatraz. The Park Rangers stationed there (Alcatroopers) make a cold ROCK, warm again.

And to Frank Heaney, former Alcatraz guard, and one of my very best friends.

I love you all . . .

# *Rap Sheet*

UNITED STATES
PENITENTIARY

ALCATRAZ ISLAND AREA 12 ACRES
1½ MILES TO TRANSPORT DOCK
ONLY GOVERNMENT BOATS PERMITTED
OTHERS MUST KEEP OFF 200 YARDS
NO ONE ALLOWED ASHORE
WITHOUT A PASS

In 1934 a warning . . . today it's a welcome . . .

*Chapter 1*

# This Ain't The Dixie Flyer

A passenger aboard the U. S. Prison Train, in transit for Alcatraz, does not ride in the luxury of your every day traveler. But, considering we were thought of as animals, Prison Officials felt it was only right that we were treated as such.

I sat there, leg irons rattling against my ankles, cold, hard, torturing. My hands were cuffed to a waist chain, hooked up to the man sharing my seat. We sat there; the seat was old, torn and faded leather. The coach we road in should have been salvaged after World War I. We resembled clowns, dressed in baggy coveralls with U.S. Prisoner stenciled up both legs and across the back.

There were two coaches (cattle cars) twenty-six cons in each. We had nothing to do but think, cuss out the world and endure the unbearable heat. But, this was part of their game plan, a ploy to break your spirit. This cargo was not run of the mill; these were convicts that knew no rules. We were the misfits of the Federal Prison system: killers, kidnapers and bank robbers. The trouble makers Uncle Sam did not even make an attempt to program into his system. Hard cases all. We had to be under twenty-four hour surveillance, or *good-bye*, we'd be gone . . . over the wall, under the wall or through the wall. It made no difference how we escaped, just so we escaped . . . .

It was a hot summer night, June, 1953. Fifty-two of the toughest cons in the nation were riding in hell, but hell was still down the track, twelve acres of hell. Alcatraz!

At each end of the coach, was a cage constructed of tempered, steel bars, a prison within a prison. In the cage, an armed guard sat upright; he cradled a wicked looking 30-30 across his lap. At his hip hung an Army issue .45. I think this was meant to discourage us. It was not exactly a tour through the Grand Canyon. I can't help joking while writing this. It seemed so unreal. Here was this guy in a cage, watching us every minute of the day, eyes squinting, waiting for us to attack. Had I been him, I would have went to sleep, we were not about to do anything, but, the guard did not know that. He had been trained to watch us *animals*, and, at no time let his guard down. Good advice, I reasoned, but a little too extreme. Throughout the history of the Prison Train, no one escaped. But, I guess there was always a first time. Years earlier, an escape attempt was made from the Kansas City train station by Frank Nash. There was a shoot-out and several guards were killed. Nash did not get to go home for supper that night, either. They called it the *Kansas City Massacre*. I assumed this tidbit was burned into each prison guard's brain while he was in training, and, again, I say, very good advice.

The entrance to the guard's cage was on the outside platform of the coach. Each guard would stand an eight-hour shift, and then another sleepy-bored face would appear, strap on the .45 and go into his act. And, an act it was. These prison train *hacks*\* were usually in the autumn of their careers and were assigned the least dangerous of assignments until they came up for retirement. Never the less, they appeared to be alert at all times and did their jobs. Once a year they made the prison train trip, and then it was back to the prison wall tower and more boredom.

The interior of the coach consisted of beat-up seats with shiny, worn out chain bolts. The windows were barred and had not been washed or opened in decades. If these windows could speak, they would tell you of other faces in the past: Al Capone, "Scar Face"(you didn't call him that to his face); George "Machine Gun" Kelly (he gave the Federal Agents the name, G-Man); and Public Enemy Number One, Alvin Karpis. All dead now, except old Creepy, Alvin Karpis. He was still on the rock and I looked forward to meeting him. He had been locked up for longer than I've been on this earth. I'm

\* *A guard the inmates respected. He was fair.*

twenty-four and old Creepy had been looking out of those bars for a long time, but 48 hours on this hot box was almost as bad.

Ventilation was poor, the air was foul and there was only one toilet for twenty-six men. Each time a man had to go to the john, he had to be uncuffed from his waist chain, and, in his leg irons, he was waddled down the aisle like a duck. It was no simple task for guard or inmate. The guards would use the same toilet. It was then, when grandpa in the cage would stand up and move the 30-30 from side to side. I think he was trying to tell us something.

They served three meals a day from the train's galley: ham and egg sandwich for breakfast, grilled cheese at lunch and for din din, a bowl of chili and oyster crackers. The coffee was first class and you could have all you wanted. Cigarettes were passed out to the men after each meal. We were told there would be no smoking after the supper meal was completed. This rule was completely ignored and there was smoking all night long. The guards just turned their backs on it; what they could not see, they could not enforce. It was their way of showing a little kindness, or, on the other hand, maybe, they did not want a small riot on their choo, choo train. This would not look too good on their trip report, either.

### "We Get Some Fresh Air"

Joe Ballard sat across the aisle from me, he was next to the window. He was a big man, ex-marine and he had seen action at Guadalcanal. You could not say he was ugly and you could not say he was pretty. I guess you could say, he was pretty ugly. His neck was large, like a football player and his nose was flattened from too many street fights. Joe's head was clean shaven and glowed from the bright lights over head. His coverall was stiff from dried blood. The left side of his head sported a large bandage completely saturated in dried blood. On the first night out from Leavenworth, Joe had asked the guard to open the window for some fresh air. Simple request. But the guard only growled back, "This ain't the Dixie Flyer, boy. The window stays closed."

Joe's hands were cuffed to his waist chain and he could not bring them above his chest. Unable to get to the window with his hands, he did the next best thing. He slammed the side of his head against the window. There was a resounding crash and there was broken glass scattered all over Joe and the wide-eyed man chained next to him.

"What the hell!" the guard yelled. "You nuts?"

Joe did not say a word, he just looked out of the broken window and took in a deep breath of the Kansas night.

Like a child, the guard was frustrated. He had been reprimanded and did not know how to handle it. "You're in trouble now," he said with a voice that lacked authority.

"Golly," I said sheepishly. "We're in trouble fellas."

The guard turned to me swiftly, "What did you say?"

"I said screw you, man. That's what I said." Our eyes locked in combat. No way was this guy going to back me down, and he knew it.

"You say we're in trouble. Man, you make me sick. How much trouble can a guy be in? We're not in trouble, you dip stick, *we are* the trouble."

His courage was returning and I expected a rap to the head from his blackjack. I held my head high to give him a good shot. It never came and I let out my breath. He seemed to relent and said softly, "I am not to be addressed as man. Please address me as officer."

I was not going to back off. Didn't he say I was in trouble. What did I have to lose. I let him have it. "You're right pal, man is a compliment. My mistake."

He took a pen and pad from out of his trouser pocket. He resembled an old gun fighter going for his hog leg. Leaning down he copied the number that was stenciled on my back, reholstered his pad and pen and scoffed off grumbling, "You're in trouble."

The endless plains of Kansas raced past the dirt-splattered windows. Breakfast was over and the last puff of smoke drifted to the ceiling. I drank the last of my coffee and retreated to my only sanctuary, sleep . . . like vampires, we slept in the daytime, and talked through the night. Somehow, the Gods that watch over convicts did a good deed. Old "You're in Trouble" was transferred to the cage and no longer walked the coach. In a way it was a shame, we had no one to pick on. I missed the son-of-a-bitch like I'd miss a toothache or a kick in the head.

The new guard on duty was a decent hack. His hair was gray, tiny blue eyes smiled at you when he talked and his voice was soft. No chip on his shoulder; this man had class. Harassment was not in his make-up. He put out extra coffee, and if you had a cigarette left over from supper, he'd let you light up.

"You're in Trouble" was completely ignored and it drove him crazy. Every three hours he'd be let out of the cage to inspect the chains. He'd walk down the aisle, lean over the seat, grab the chain of the man sitting there and give it a good jerk. This hurt, but the man didn't give him the satisfaction of crying out. Each time he made his rounds we all made an effort to smile at him. We felt we owed him that much and, boy, did that drive him crazy; "You're in Trouble" was in trouble. To the cons, "You're in Trouble" was classified as a *screw*.* He was an individual given minor authority with the ambition to be in command. His main goal in life was to be promoted to sergeant. The average screw had only one way of doing things, his way. When the cards were dealt to the screw, it was a stacked deck. He was a robot, predictable, easy to read. Through the years the screw would take test after test to make the grade of sergeant. He would finally make it (he had to) for he knew every question and answer by memory. But now politics would enter the equation; the screw would be passed over and some young man in the ranks, who was better material and had potential, would take his place on the roster. "You're in Trouble" did not fit. He was not the caliber to become sergeant. The convicts knew this and so did the Bureau of Prisons. Consequently, the screw would ride the rails for thirty years or do some other menial job, be given a gold-filled

---

* *Considered lower than whale crap and that's at the bottom of the ocean.*

watch and be put out to pasture with the rest of the mushrooms.

There are three rungs to the ladder: the officer, the hack and the screw. An officer will approach things with an open mind. As a rule, he will allow the inmate to tell his story, and he would check out the facts and make judgment. Sometimes it went for you, sometimes it did not, but, at least, you got a fair trial. An officer had the ability to evaluate the nature of the man. The screw did not even know how to put his pants on right. Then there's the hack, usually the ol' timer just putting in his days until retirement. He was often put into the position of instructor in a trade shop. He was still a guard, but he would not go out of his way to make your life miserable. There was no pettiness in his makeup. He let you do your time and he did his. If the occasion called for it, such as a murder or an escape attempt, he would stand by his comrades and would attack you with everything he could muster. We all knew this and we respected it.

The rails sang, click-it-de-click, click-it-de-clack and the train raced across the endless, flat plains. Soon we would be in the foothills and then the mountains. The next day, the broad Pacific and Alcatraz. The end of the line. . .

I glanced over at Frazer, the man I was chained up with. He was in his early twenties. A quiet guy from Philadelphia. We had talked for about fifteen minutes on the trip so far. . . where we were from, how much time we had and what we got it for. Unlike some, Frazer did not proclaim his innocence. He was guilty, but his sentence did not fit the crime. Here was a young man who parlayed a thirty-day sentence into a thirty-year sentence. He had been in the army taking basic training and decided he wanted to go home for the weekend. The fence around the camp was not very high so he took off. Three days later he was picked up in Philadelphia by the Military Police and was being returned to camp. They never made it. Somehow Frazer had worked himself loose from his bounds, grabbed the driver of the car around the neck and caused the vehicle to crash. The driver was killed in the escape attempt and Frazer received a sentence of thirty years at his General Court Martial.

Frazer was sleeping now, a deep sleep. His snoring bounced off the coach walls. I pulled the chain sharply. Frazer's eyes popped open. "Huh, what?"

"Wake up, Kenny. You're rattling the bars again." That was the understatement of the year. This guy could be heard clear back in Philadelphia.

"Okay, Okay. Gee's, a guy can't get any sleep in this box car." "When you sleep, nobody sleeps." I was talking to myself, Frazer was snoring again.

I leaned over and looked up and down the aisle, nodded to a few of the guys I knew from Leavenworth and then returned to my thinking. My thoughts were sour, two more days of this with nothing to do. but just look at each other, crack a joke that was not funny under the circumstances and cuss out "You're in Trouble."

*Chapter 2*

## One For The Ol' Man

I tried going over events in my life that were pleasant, but found this difficult. Life was not pleasant during the great depression; it was a dog-eat-dog world. There were no handouts, you fought for what you got and you held on tight. I was born on the south side of Chicago in the County Hospital on October 31st, 1927. You guessed it, Halloween. I was a twelve-pound baby, the first for my mother. I gave her a bad time at my birth and continued to do so until the day she died. The quote, "You're going to drive me to an early grave," was meant for the likes of me. I loved my mother dearly, but something in me, a rebellious Dr. Hyde, brought out all the bad in me. I can find no one to blame for this. My dad was the greatest, but we were not that close until later years. When I was a kid I can remember three occasions he took me someplace: the Chicago Worlds Fair, a movie showing the "Fighting 69th", and one trip to the beach. Not a big brother type father would you say? He was okay though. I guess when you're out hustling a living for your family you haven't got too much time or money for entertainment. I remember vividly how he would come home every night covered with coal dust; he looked like a raccoon. He worked twelve hours a day driving a truck and shoveling coal at $.50 an hour.

In the summer it was just the opposite. He delivered ice to homes in the neighborhood, hauling fifty-pound blocks up three and four flights of winding stairs. A large leather patch covered the right shoulder to protect it from freezing. He worked the neighborhood for eight hours and at night he delivered five-hundred-pound blocks to the dairies in the area. He would stop at home for supper and then go on his dairy route. He often took me along for the ride and to help push the long blocks of ice down the chutes. I always enjoyed making these trips with my father. Once we got the ice sliding down the chutes, I would hop aboard and ride it down like an ice horse. The men who worked for the dairy were always decent to us and gave dad and I a package on the way out. I think other than the men who worked for the dairy, we were the only family in the neighborhood who had all the eggs, butter and milk we could handle. What a country, huh?

Life really stunk during the great depression and being born on the south side of Chicago was not an added attraction. The south side started on 22nd Street and ended at 122nd Street. Its east and west boundaries were from State Street to Halsted Street on the west. One mile wide and ten miles deep and the toughest battleground the city could offer. Al Capone ruled supreme; he ran the rackets. Every Italian family I knew in my neighborhood made *dago red** for Al's taverns and brothels. The hard stuff came from over the border in Canada; the softer stuff came from bath tubs. I was only twelve or thirteen at the time, but I was well educated in the streets. I grew up with Italian kids; we fought and played together and stayed at each others' houses. We were family and still are.

I was seventeen when I was released from the Chicago Parental School.

I had been housed there for one year, six months for breaking into a store (that was in reality a *fence***) and three two-month stretches for escape, the last one was two months prior to my release. I was seventeen and they had to turn me loose; it was the law.

My first bout with crime came in a strange manner. My dad, as I have mentioned, was a truck driver. One day, while driving a load of ice on the outskirts of Chicago, he was involved in an accident. He slammed into a car at a blind intersection, killing one person and injuring two others. Dad was

*home brewed red wine*
**A person who bought stolen goods.*

hauled off to jail and accused of manslaughter. He had a $1000.00 bond, and they just as well could have made it a million; my dad had never seen $1000.00 altogether in his entire lifetime, more or less on that day in court. He was forced to stay in the County Jail for three weeks before his first court appearance and God only knew how long after that. But, I didn't wait for God. I was only sixteen, but I knew a few moves, and I meant to use them. It didn't take a big brain to figure that Stan's Grocery Store would be a good hit. I had played penny ante poker in his back room many times and I knew the whole layout. This guy was a small-time fence, but he did a lot of business. He was a bum; he gave the local hoods less than 5 cents on the dollar for their loot, when any self-respecting fence would pay from 10 cents to 25 cents on the dollar. Stan was also short on brains. He was too cheap to install an alarm or even to get a dog. He did not trust banks and kept his money in the store. There was no doubt other people were casing his store, but it was apparent they did not know where he kept his goodies. There was one person who did, yours truly.

I never thought about it at the time, but every day on my way to school, at about eight-thirty in the morning, I stopped at Stan's to pick up my daily ration of candy. Stan was often at the door opening up for the day's business as I arrived. He would let me in, I'd purchase my candy and be on my way to school. Sometimes I'd give him a quarter for 10 cents worth of candy and he'd give me the change out of the cash register. The coins he handed me were freezing cold. Oh, yes, I knew where he hid his money.

My dad had been in jail for about three days when I decided to make my move. I did not use any cat burglar tactics, I just watched Stan close up for the evening. It was still early so I took in the movie at the local theater. After the movie, when the crowd thinned out, I strolled past Stan's. There was a little night light hanging in the middle of the store. I walked past Stan's and down to the corner, did an about face and headed back. It was so quiet I could hear my heart pounding; to say I was scared would be an understatement, I think I wet my pants. But regardless, Stan's was going to go. And it was now. Next to Stan's store, on the sidewalk, Stan had placed two empty milk cases. I put them both through the glass front door and headed directly for the freezer. Three minutes later I was walking down the alley heading for my house. In my hands were three cigar boxes, cold cigar boxes, filled with money. My first score had netted me twenty-six hundred dollars. I went to school the next day, and on the way, I stopped at Stan's as usual. I couldn't get in, he had been robbed and there were cops all over the joint. That afternoon after school, I gave my mother the good news; I had a friend of mine that loaned me the *G-note** to get Dad out. She went for it.

But, the cops that paid us a visit around 5:00 that evening did not go for it. It was simple, now that I think of it. I had flashed money around at school, (a rule I have never broken since) they put two and two together and came up with Johnny Dekker. While at our house, they searched my room and found sixteen hundred dollars. I was quickly dispatched to the 12th District, the local police station. The next two hours were unpleasant, to say the least. I was pushed into a chair and grilled about the *prowl.*** First, one cop, and then the other, for two solid hours, one was the bad guy—"I'll break your head guy"—the other was the good guy—"Come on, Steve, take it easy on the kid, he'll tell us all about it, won't you Johnny?" These guys put Laurel and Hardy to shame, but at the time I did not think it was so funny. I honestly believe the bad guy was about to knock me out of the chair and walk all over my bones. While I was being questioned one of them left the room; he returned in about ten minutes with a finger-print expert. They painted my hand black with ink and pressed it down, palm and all, onto a piece of white paper. The finger print expert took out a magnifying glass, checked the paper with my palm print and nodded.

"You got your guy," he said.

* *$1,000.00 bill.*
** *Slang for burglary.*

The good guy smiled, the bad guy smiled. "Well, John, where do we go from here?"

"Have I got a choice?" I asked.

"You've got a choice, John. There was twenty-six hundred bucks taken in that prowl of Stan's. We found sixteen hundred. What happened to the other thousand?"

I had no choice. I was not going to tell them where the other thousand went, not in this lifetime.

Sorry, guys, you got the wrong palm print. I threw up my hands to stop the blows that were surely coming, but they never came. Instead, I was picked up bodily, carried to the back room and tossed into a cell. The rest of the night, I tossed and turned to the tune of a drunk sleeping it off in the next cell. The next morning I was taken in a police van to Juvenile Detention Home, a.k.a. John Dillinger's Hotel. I was there a week before I came up for trial. All they had was the palm print, but it was enough for the judge to find me guilty and I was sentenced to six months in the Chicago Parental School.

Principally, the school was for the housing of run-aways and truants, but the judge gave me a break. He felt it would not be in the interest of justice to send a sixteen-year-old to the state penitentiary. And he made it quite clear, that if I was ever up before him again, he would throw the book at me.

The Parental School was a breeding ground for the wise guys of the future. The population consisted of mostly fifteen- and sixteen-year-olds from every neighborhood in Chicago. Tough kids, one and all.

There was the West Side Gang, the North Side Gang and the South Side Gang. The East Side Gang did not exist; if they did, they were fish from out of Lake Michigan. It was here, between math, reading and writing, that you were educated in the art of hot-wiring a car, cracking a safe or just about anything to keep a young kid from becoming bored. It was here you learned to defend yourself. You were taught only one way, that was to win. To lose a fight was not something to be ashamed of, but to back off from a battle was an invitation for every bully in the gangs to bounce your head off the wall just to work up an appetite. I think I had one hundred and one fights and won them all but a hundred. I ran away so many times that they used to say, "Don't pay any attention to him, that's Dekker and he's part of the fence." Trouble was, every time you ran away and were brought back, all the guys in the cottage beat the hell out of you, and the cottage officer would stand by and watch. I didn't stop trying though, and I did an extra six months for it. I returned to the Parental School several years later. My intentions were to bust the cottage officer's nose in. It was going to be pay-back time, but he was no longer employed there and I went on my way. It would have been a dumb move and I would have ended up in jail, but, it would have been worth it.

But this was all over now. It was 1944 and I had a whole new world to do battle with. The war was in its third year and the City of Chicago was swinging. Most of the eighteen-year-olds were out fighting a war; there were ten girls for every guy and the black market was going full throttle. I figured there was something in this for me, some scam, some way to make money without putting my tail out too far. While in the Parental School, I had managed to fill out my six-foot frame, mainly, by eating everything in sight and working on the weights in the evening. I kept my hair in a crew cut, the style that the G.I.s were blessed with in training camp. My eyes are hazel but appear blue when I am angered or provoked. I think my main problem in life, then and now, was I always had a wise crack answer for everything. I always said, if a guy stuck with me for a year, he had to be a friend. Anybody that could stand me for a year had to be a friend or was out of his cotton pickin' mind.

My friends were my friends, they were my peers and I treated them as such. There were no leaders, and I was not a follower. I endeavored to be a standup guy. I did what I wanted to, when I wanted to and never put one of my friends in jeopardy. I never talked anyone into anything they did not want to do in the first place.

14

Perhaps, I would have taken a different direction in life, but, probably not. My environment had nothing to do with it. My home life was on par with the rest of the kids in the neighborhood; they were poor, too, but they did not end up in half the jails in the country. Was it in the genes? Grandpa Dekker was a baker, he liked to make dough, maybe that's it. I was fond of dough myself, not his kind though. (Thought I'd throw a little pun in there.) The truth is, I had an over-abundance of adventure in my system; I did not like to take orders—such as employment—I hated school with a passion and what I really think led to my rebellion against society was comic books. I would read them for hours on end, especially crime comics. From these books of higher education, I visioned myself, but most of all, I attempted to find the mistakes these desperadoes made while committing crime. Ironically, enough, I made a mistake on my first *caper.** I flashed money.

I enjoyed the life I led. My only touch of a conscience was the embarrassment and hurt I brought upon my family. At fourteen I was a member of the "Derby's," a group of guys and girls who wore derby hats cocked upon their head. I had started the trend when I bought an old derby hat at a rummage sale. I wore it the next day and it caught on. Slowly, but surely, each member of the group managed to get a hat. We wore the hats everywhere we went, school, the ice cream parlor, the skating rink. The hats went where we went. But, this was over now. I was seventeen and ready to get down to business.

No one was waiting for me when I walked out of the Parental School. I had not told anyone of my release date. Why allow my mother to make that long trip across town on a streetcar? She had been making that trip every week for the last year. Rain or shine, Ma would catch the streetcar and head for the Parental School to visit her little boy, Johnny. She was a frail, tiny woman with short blonde hair and bangs. Her eyes were light blue, but perhaps, with too much mascara and had

* Criminal act.

a sad look. But, they would shine when she saw her son. She always appeared cheerful when she met me at the gate. In each hand was a shopping bag, loaded to the top with candy, pop corn and bottles of soda pop. We sat in the shade, on a bench under an old oak tree with hundreds of initials carved into it. We talked mostly of how things would change when I got home. I made it understood, that when I came home, I would not be going back to school again. I would be seventeen and I had that choice. School was out, thereby eliminating the constant quarrels with my dad. It was the only fault I could find with my ol' man, his never-ending harping about school. Other than that, he was a standup guy. I can only remember one whipping he gave me. It was the time he caught me smoking on the back staircase of the apartment building we were living in at the time. He beat the hell out of me, but from what I know about cigarettes now, he should have cut my throat.

No, Ma Dekker had taken her last streetcar ride. This day she would be in for a surprise.

I caught the streetcar east to Western Avenue, then transferred south. It was a two-hour trip to the south side; it was stop and go every two blocks. On the way, at Belmont and Western, was Riverview, Chicago's amusement park. It was two-cent day and people were waiting in long lines; no ride cost more than two cents. It was early and the lines were not too long, later in the day it would be a rat race. To me it seemed like every other couple had a man in uniform with a girl hanging onto his arm. "Have fun now," I thought. "Some of you might never come back."

At Forty-third Street, I transferred east over to Halsted, then south again toward home. Cattle trucks were lined up and down Halsted Street, waiting to enter the stock yards. It was still early and the wind had not kicked up yet, but when it did, God help the people in the direction the wind was blowing. At the present I was saying a little prayer myself . . .

My mother greeted me at the door with a cry of happiness and look of disapproval.

She hugged me. "Why didn't you tell me you were coming home?" Her face showed alarm. "Did you run away again?" She held me close.

I encircled her in my arms and picked her up off the steps. "Nah, Ma, I'm home for good. They even gave me a diploma saying I graduated from high school."

"But, Johnny, you were only in the tenth grade. How did you do it, did you get double promoted?"

"Sure did, Ma, bet you didn't think you had such a smart son."

I waved the diploma in front of her, teasing her. She tried grabbing for it but I held it high over my head. I didn't feel so smart now. She was so happy and I was such a con artist. No harm done, though. She'd never know the truth anyway. I did not exactly lie to my mother, I just stretched the truth a little. If I had told her I had the diploma made up in the school print shop the day before my release, it would have broken her heart. I'm glad she didn't get her hands on that diploma, the print was still wet.

"Kids in school?" I asked going up the steps and through the door into the kitchen.

"Yes," she answered scampering past me. "And, as you can see, the house is a mess." She began to take dishes from the kitchen table and pile them into the sink, embarrassed at the supper pans on the stove, probably from the night before. She turned to me and said, "I guess I'll have to get Minny over here to tidy up a bit. I just can't find time for it all."

It was a five-room house built in the back near the alley. In the front was a half acre of lush, green grass. It was cut exactly two inches high from one end to the other. This was my father's pet project. Every night he would water it after sunset and run the lawn mower over it once a week on Saturday. Directly in front of the house were two pear trees, on the side of the lot were two cherry trees. The house once belonged to my grandmother and grandfather. Both being from the old country, they knew how to use the land. Mom and dad were not quite the pioneer type, and if it was not for my father, there would be a baseball diamond in the front yard.

When grandma and grandpa passed away they left the house to my mother and uncle Fred. My father and uncle Fred got together and agreed to buy one or the other out. At that time, they figured the house was worth in the neighborhood of $20,000. Unfortunately, uncle Fred and my father, financially speaking, did not reside in that neighborhood. Dad was just a working man at the Sherwin Williams Paint Co. His modest pay was just enough to take care of the rent and keep food on the table for three children. Uncle Fred never did hold down a steady job, he fancied himself a pool shark and made his money hustling marks in the pool rooms throughout Chicagoland.

Somewhere, along the line, uncle Fred had forgotten how to swim and lost more games than he won. So, dad bought uncle Fred out for $10,000. They drew up the papers and held a party in celebration. As agreed, dad paid uncle Fred $5,000 down, money dad borrowed from grandpa Dekker, and paid uncle Fred $75.00 a month, no interest. Uncle Fred had insisted on that. He might have been a shark at pool, but he was a tadpole at business. It was a small house, just five rooms, but it was theirs. My mother was not the best housekeeper in the world, but she had the greatest *scam* * in the world and could pay for a woman to come in and clean the house once or twice a week.

At the beginning of the depression, when dad worked for 50 cents an hour, Madam Dekker began her career at reading fortunes for women in the neighborhood. Soon, by way of mouth, Madam Dekker was known all over the south side. She would take appointments over the phone and, on occasion, read for groups. She charged 50 cents per reading and usually brought in fifteen to twenty dollars a day, tax free.

There was no trick to telling fortunes, nothing mystic. People who believe in fortune telling tend to expose their trouble freely during conversation with the fortune teller, and

* *Confidence game*

all Ma had to do, was fill in the details and make the mark feel better. If their love life was bad, you tell them it was on the upswing; if their money was low, don't worry, dear, according to the cards things would pick up at work and you will be looking at some property in the near future. And I hear wedding bells! They loved it; they ate it up and they told their friends, and, above all, they came back for more.

Ma once told me my fortune. But, it was not con this time. She was serious. "Johnny," she said, "I see in the cards that someday you will sit in the electric chair." There were tears in her eyes. With a sweep of her hand she scattered the cards all over the floor. I got up from the table, bent over and picked up the cards and then took her into my arms in a big bear hug. I laughed in her ear.

"Ma, you're full of beans, and I love ya."

The party began just after school let out. Billy my younger brother let out a yell as he walked into the kitchen. I stood up and we jumped into each others arms with a thud. Billy was six years younger than me and our thud knocked him to the floor. He jumped up quickly and went into a boxer's stance. He was no Joe Louis, that was for sure. He was six inches shorter than me and chubby. I put my hand on his head and kept him at a distance, at the same time I ruffled up his hair; it looked like it had not been combed in a week. I let him swing punches in the air for a minute and then turned him loose.

"How ya doing, Bill?"

"Gee, it's been almost a year since I seen ya last, John. You didn't break out did ya?"

His eyes were wide open when I answered him. "Sorry, Bill, you can't tell the kids at school I busted out again. Besides, you don't break out of joints like that. You walk away, maybe a little fast, but you walk away. It's not like a prison. The old goats that run the joint couldn't stop to take a pee, much less, stop a guy from getting out."

Billy appeared a little disappointed at this disclosure. He looked up to me and someday hoped to be like me. There was always excitement in his brother's life; Johnny was a guy you could count on. He was the leader of the Derbys. He said he wasn't, but he was, because when Johnny said, "Jump!", they said, "How high?" He was popular, he had chicks knocking down the door, and you can bet, he was not a virgin. "Gee's," he thought, "why couldn't he have broken out? What the hell am I gunna tell the guys now?"

Toots, my sister, was next to greet me. She was short, robust and full of life. Her blond hair was cut in the style of Veronica Lake, the movie queen. Her hair covered one eye, like a sleeve of gold, with a blue eye looking out. She was a year younger than me, in her second year of high school and just beginning to realize boys were different than girls. She thought of me as a hoodlum; always fighting, always running away from home and always selecting her boy friends. I thought that's what big brothers were for, to keep jerks like me away. But, she always told me, Mind your own bee's wax.

I gave Toots a peck on the lips. I neglected to hug her, as she had grown since I had last seen her, and I felt embarrassed. Little Tootie was growing up and soon I would have to be giving her boxing lessons for the wolves of Fanger High. I knew what these guys were after and the guy that got it was going to have to be one hell of a guy, because Toots, regardless of how she acted, was no push over. And then, too, if the guy wasn't right, I'd handle it my way.

It was like old times, the four of us sitting there on the porch. Only one person was missing, my father. He was working overtime. With the war on, they needed a lot of paint for the tanks, planes and ships; sort of like an Indian war party, lots of paint.

Shortly before six p.m., my father showed up. He parked his old 1937 Ford out on the street, close to the sidewalk, leading back to the house. The car was glossy black with large white sidewalls. It was my dad's pride and joy; he washed it once a week and kept it in excellent mechanical condition. There was over one hundred and twenty thousand miles on the engine and it purred like a kitten. He often bragged, that if he had to drive to the West Coast, his car would make it—

no trouble. Walking down the sidewalk in long strides I could see where I got my height. My dad stood six feet, or better. His shoulders were broad and his chest was deep. His blond hair was thinning and a sign of gray appeared at his temples. I pictured myself in twenty years. I'd go for that. Dad squinted his eyes when he saw me. He raised both of his arms, as if in prayer, and hoped for the best. Johnny, you didn't run off again, did you?

I shook his hand and gave him a kiss on the lips—so I'm weak it was a long moment before I answered. "No, Dad, I got my walking papers this time. You don't have to hide me."

While in the Parental School, I had jumped the fence three times, came home and was picked up each time by the same police officers, in the same squad car. They pulled up in a cloud of dust and screeching tires. It was really keystone cop action. I never attempted to run, but I guess they did not know that. So, they brought me back, so what? I'd run away again. I had no intentions of making it easy for the establishment. Lock me up if I committed a crime, that's business. But, don't lock me up for ditching school, that's bush league. They could lock me up, but the first chance I got, I'd play rabbit on them.

*Chapter 3*

## "The Sting"

Old habits are hard to break and it took me a week before I could manage to sleep for twelve hours straight. Reform school does that to you. . . in bed at 9 p.m., up at 6 a.m., lousy schedule to live by. Have you any idea what it's like to be up early in the morning like that? And do you know there are actually people out and about? Probably a crew of burglars just getting home. Don't tell me vampires, I don't believe in that garbage.

After three months, I finally broke away from the *Derbys* and began to hang around West Pullman. There was a pool room there, my uncle Fred worked in, sweeping the floors, brushing the tables, and playing gopher for the guys at the poker table. He was getting old and no longer had his stroke. He couldn't win any money in the pool room, so he went to work for them. I knew how he felt, going to work. Gee's!!! . . .

I just hung around and got to know the guys. It was better than sitting at home, and just from watching, I began to learn the game of poker. It was a small game, a 50-cent limit, and usually the same guys played every night. At one time or another I stood behind every player and studied his game. You learn a lot like this: who bluffs, who plays close to the belt and who doesn't know how to play at all. I played my first game on a Saturday night and found out quick, I was one of those that could not play at all. I had to walk home at night, street cars did not take I.O.U.s. I gave up poker for a living after that. My next venture was betting on the horses. This was going to be a snap; the money was going to come in now! Hell, anybody can pick one horse out of a six-horse field. While I'm thinking about this, you know, they should make up a rule:

when a jockey comes in last, they should shoot him. That way, all the jockeys would really be trying.

I think I'm the only guy at the bookie that bet on a match race and lost. The local bookie was next door to the pool hall, in a barber shop. It was my second home and it was here I met Dugan. The bookie was Dugan's first home. He was there to catch the first races coming in from New York, and stayed till the last race out of California. He could tell you by reading the *Racing Form* just how a horse would run that particular race: this was a speed horse, this was a closer, he knew it all. Dugan was the guy I got the tip from for the match race.

What I liked most about Dugan was his sense of humor. This guy never bitched about anything. If he lost on a horse, he'd pound his forehead with the palm of his hand, or, if he was sitting at a bar, he'd rap it with his forehead. (I saw a guy do that in Las Vegas once, and I had to walk up to see if it was Dugan.)

Across the street from the bookie was a hamburger joint. Dugan ate there once in a while, so I started to run over there with him. On one occasion, as we ate, I mentioned I had been in the Parental School and had been out for three months. He was surprised to hear I had served time for burglary, and I was surprised I had told him. The discussion did not last long. We went back to talking about the horses.

Dugan was only eighteen, short with brown hair, a blue-eyed Irishman that liked fast women and slow horses. He had avoided the draft because of a punctured eardrum, and, I think, a flat forehead.

One Saturday, while eating burgers and fries with Dugan, he came up with a scam to beat the bookie. I was all ears, at last, some action. Our bookie, the barber shop, was on 120th Street. There was also another bookie on 123rd and Halsted, a much bigger bookie with a lot more action.

The bookie on 123rd Street got the results and the call of the race directly from the Organization, the *People*, the *Outfit*, whatever you want to call them, and placed the results of the race on a large sheet of paper on the wall.

"You do know how to read?" he asked, jokingly.

I nodded.

"Good."

It wasn't good, it was great, simple and great. He explained that our mark was a bit on the greedy side and always took bets up to the last minute from the players in the barber shop. Dugan was only a ten dollar better and he said the score might not be big, but if we pulled off two races, we'd have a nice score.

I didn't give a damn, I was willing to go along with anything, and this sounded like a sure thing.

We needed another guy to make the plan work, so Dugan got on the phone. He talked for about a minute and came back to the booth smiling.

"We got our guy, Johnny boy," he was very excited. "He'll be here in twenty minutes. His name is Bob Kline, you'll like him, he's cool."

Bob got there in about five minutes. He was driving an old Model A Ford. He was in his twenties and served with the Merchant Marine, as a deck hand on the iron ore boats that sailed Lake Michigan. This was considered active duty, even though he was not in a war zone.

We were lucky to catch him between shipments. He was usually out to sea, or in this case, "out to lake." I talked to him for about five minutes, and I loved this guy. Everything he did was with an air of confidence; his walk was cocky, when he spoke, he knew what he was talking about, and when he listened, he did not miss a word. He was extremely good looking, he knew it, but did not put on airs. His hair was curly, with a cowlick. His eyes were brown, maybe a little sad. His teeth were white and even they were enhanced by his deep tan. He was a country boy from Iowa, but he was street wise and the big city was where he wanted to be.

There were only the three of us in the hamburger joint. Mike, the owner, was up at the front cleaning the grill. Dugan figured we were safe talking, so he laid out the plan. He told us that he had read the *Racing Form* earlier in the day for the races at Arlington Park, and we were going to *past post* * two races. Each race was a six-horse event, no complications that way; a twelve-horse field could be nothing but trouble, too many ways to screw up. Our first race would be going off at three p.m., it was the fifth race. Dugan would be in the barber shop; he would bet $10.00 on the first four races, all $10.00 exactas. If we won, that was great, but exactas are hard to pick and we expected to lose. Dugan would sit there, reading the *Racing Form* and picking his horses. Swede, the man that ran the bookie, would know Dugan had been there all day and would not suspect a thing. My job was to be in the bookie on 123rd Street when the fifth race was run, get the results and phone them back to Bob in the hamburger joint. I was there when the fifth race went off; the number two horse won the race, and the five-horse came in second. I left quickly and went right to the phone. It rang one time and Bob answered.

"Two, five," I said, and hung up.

Bob took out a package of cigarettes, emptied it out on the table and replaced two cigarettes. He then took a book of matches, tore all of them out but five, placed the package of cigarettes and book of matches in his shirt pocket and went directly to the bookie. He waved at the other fellas sitting around and asked for a *Racing Form*. Dugan handed him his.

"Got a hot one, Bob?" he asked.

"Na, just thought I'd try something with a pretty name," Bob replied.

"Got a smoke?" Dugan asked.

Bob reached into his shirt and took out the package of cigarettes, handed them to Dugan and began to read the *Racing Form*.

Dugan took a cigarette and handed the package back to Bob. "You got a match?" he asked.

Bob handed him the matches. "How you fixed for shoes?" he joked.

Dugan got down to business. He took a ten dollar bill from out of his wallet and tossed it across the table to Swede.

* *Bet on a horse after he has won*

"Give me a ten dollar exacta on the two and five in the fifth, Swede." Dugan held his breath in anticipation.

Swede did not waste a second, he took out his pad and wrote the numbers two and five for Dugan. We got him!

The exacta paid two hundred and seventeen dollars. The book's limit on the exacta payoff was two hundred and two dollars. When Swede got the results on the fifth race he looked sick, but he paid off like a cash register. "Dugan picks another winner." he said without much gusto.

"No kidding!" Dugan said, trying to look excited. "How much did I get?"

"One thousand, ten bucks!" Swede said, handing the money to Dugan. "Now, maybe, you can get a haircut," he laughed.

Dugan pocketed the money without counting it and returned the laugh. "No, thank you, Swede, I'd rather let my girl friend give me a haircut with a bowl, than get chopped up by you." Dugan had to rub it in, "Especially after winning all this dough from you, you'd probably chop my ears off, and I can't hear now." He pulled a wad of cotton from out of his right ear. "That's why I'm 4-F, case you ever wondered about it."

Dugan was getting excited and hostile. Bob watched him and wondered what the hell was going on.

Dugan nodded to Bob, "Come on, let's get the hell out of this joint. I don't like sore losers."

Bob followed Dugan out the door and they walked to his car in silence. Bob started the car and, as they pulled away from the curb, Dugan broke into a laugh. "We got the Swede good, didn't we?"

"Sure did. Got him good, but what the hell did you get mad about?"

"I wasn't mad, I just wanted to get out of there. We don't need to bet the next race. We made about nine hundred clear. That's enough for today. Now, let's head over and pick up Johnny."

*Chapter 4*

# "One More Time"

I can't figure it out, but I must have aura about me that says, "How do you do? I am a crook. Would you like to work with me?"

Anyway, that's how it seems to me. No matter where I go, I always end up with the shady people of the world, and, sooner or later, I'm into something that's not quite within the statutes of the law, and not honest, either. Take Bob, Dugan and me. I knew Dugan for about a month; Bob, for five minutes. And, before the day was over, I was three hundred bucks richer.

To coin a phrase from the late Al Capone, "Boids ofa feder, flock ta gether." Who am I to dispute these words of wisdom? People that did usually got their heads caved in with a baseball bat, and Al had a better batting record than Babe Ruth.

I had dreams that this relationship between Dugan, Bob and I would work into a good source of income, but as it usually happens, Murphy's Law came upon the scene in the form of the female gender. Dugan had a girl friend named Vi, a cute brunette (I think, because she always wore a babushka with bangs hanging out.) She had a trim figure and worked in a bank. Maybe, that's why Dugan was going with her. He probably thought he could get some free samples. Bob was courting a gal named, Kay Kay. That woman loved herself so much she had people call her by her first name twice. I did not think too much of her. She was pretty, no doubt about that, but she was overly conceited, and flirting was her long suit. Other than that, I guess she was okay. Me, I had the newspaper. Dugan had Vi, Bob had Kay Kay and I had the Chicago *Sun Times*.

We began hanging out at a place called the Normal Grill. It was a gathering spot for the after-movie crowd. Across the street from the grill was the Normal Theater, which was across the street from the Normal Florist and that was across the street from the Normal Drug Store. This was obviously a co-incidence. The grill was a swinging place after the last show let out. The juke box carried the latest hits and was constantly going. On one side of the grill was a counter, on the other side was a line of booths. After the movie, you could not find a place to sit. The guy who owned it had a gold mine and he didn't even have to blow a hole in the ground. His name was Sheik, and it fit him to a tee. He was tall, well groomed and good looking.

This was a guy that had to fight off the girls, young and old, 16 or 60. Only problem was, the Sheik was gay and had eyes for Bob. See what I mean by Murphy's Law?

Dugan, Bob and I always sat in a back booth with the girls. This was good in a way because my paper did not take up much room. One night I must have been daydreaming—can you daydream at night?—anyway, Dugan picks my paper up and taps me on the head.

"You okay?" he asked.

"Yeah, why?"

"Well, you've been here two whole minutes and you haven't made a wise crack yet."

"I was just thinking about you, Dugan."

"Yeah."

"Yeah, I was thinking how proud I am of you. You really have will power." I had him thinking now. "Yeah. You know, you haven't bet a horse in three weeks. And, I was thinking about another joint just like the Swede's. It's on Michigan Avenue. You stay in there for a couple of days, Dugan, like you did at the Swede's, and I'll bet you can pick another exacta like you did last time."

I really had his attention now. I could almost hear the gears turning in his head. He was calculating the cost. I saved him the trouble.

"Three days, fifty bucks a day, hundred and fifty bucks, and then I know you'll pick a winner."

The girls had no idea what I was talking about, but Dugan and I did.

Dugan looked to Bob. "You going to be around in three days, sailor?"

"That depends on Kay Kay." He placed his hand over her shoulder and gave her a gentle squeeze. "What do you think, honey, will Bob Bob be around?"

She took his hand and moved it to her breast. "Bob Bob better be with Kay Kay."

"I'll be here." he said to Dugan.

You know, I would have bet he'd say that.

The next day we all tossed in fifty dollars apiece to make the bankroll to cover three days of betting. Let me say here and now, Dugan could not pick his nose. He lost fifteen races in a row and the bookie loved him. On the forth day, the romance was over. We made our play. There was one slight variation; I had suggested to Dugan the night before we were to make our bets, that instead of betting two races for the day—which could be a disaster—why don't we make two bets on the same race. We would make one bet on the exacta and one bet on the *quinalla*.* He ate my idea up. I was a genius, he said. I didn't agree with him out loud, but I knew that.

Day number four came and we were out one hundred and fifty, as expected. The way things were arranged now, we would have to come up with an additional $100. No problem. I still had money left over from the last score, so I tossed it into the pot. Dugan had bought a *Racing Form* earlier that morning and we decided on race number five. It was a wide open affair with no clear cut favorite. Our game plan was the same as last time; me at the bookie on 123rd Street, Bob in a laundromat, just down the block from the bookie.

The bookie got his butt kicked that day, and so did Murphy's Law. Everything went according to plan. The exacta paid $213.60 and the quinalla a whopping $190.40. We pulled in

* *Quinalla: Pick the first and second horse; either way, you win.*

$1956.00 on a twenty dollar bill. We cleared seventeen hundred and six dollars, after taking out the two hundred and fifty up front money.

While we were splitting up the money, later in the day, I made another suggestion to Dugan. "I don't know how you guys feel about it," I began, making sure Bob was listening, "but I think we better put this scam to bed for a while. No use pushing our luck. Agreed?"

"I'll go for that," Bob said, while counting his money.

"But . . ." Dugan seemed confused.

"No but's, Dugan!" It was the first time I ever showed authority in my voice toward Dugan. "How long do you think we can get away with this? These people aren't idiots, word will get around and then they will lay for you. And when they catch you in the scam, you'll come out of it with the big exacta, two broken legs."

"John, you're right. I was going to suggest the same thing."

*Chapter 5*

## "Let's Fix Daddy"

I was still living at home and it was beginning to take its toll on me. Everyday there was pressure on me, stupid things, like, "You'll have to go to work if you don't go to school." Thanks Dad. "He's too young to go to work. He goes to school." Right Ma.

I made up my mind to move in with Dugan and Bob. They had a little place on 120th, two bedrooms, a small kitchen, a bathroom and toilet the size of a phone booth. Dugan called it, 718; that's because it was located at 718 West 120th Street. I managed to convince my dad that it was best I move. Ma was a different story. She wanted to know about this Dugan fellah, what did he do for a living, how old was he, why wasn't he in the war? Finally, she gave in and I moved out that afternoon. I think what sold her on the idea was I told her Dugan was in the book business.

Well, that was not a lie. Dugan did do a lot of business with the books.

The next six weeks were a little on the boring side. Bob had gone out on an ore boat and would be away for at least three trips. He sailed between Chicago and Duluth, Minnesota as a deck hand and made us a promise this would be his last voyage. There was two reasons for this. One, Kay was pregnant. Two, if they had a baby, he would not have to worry about being drafted. So Dugan and I just waited until Bob's return. Then things picked up, got real exciting. Bob wrecked his Model A, when a parked car ran into him while he had been drinking. And golly, I met a girl at the Normal Grill.

I had noticed her sitting with a guy at the counter earlier in the week and liked what I saw, but being the shy fella that I am, I did not make a play. I did ask Vi if she knew the girl, though, and was happy to hear they were old school mates. I let it go at that for the time being because I knew in my diabolic mind, that sooner than later Vi would tell the girl I was asking about her and then we would let nature take its course. Sure enough, Helen, that was her name, started playing the juke-box, which was next to the booth we occupied. She was a very pretty girl with shoulder length brown hair; her complexion showed very little makeup and her eyes were green with a slight slant to them. On one of her trips to the juke-box, she appeared to be having a difficult time making her selection, and the longer she stood there, the more I wanted to meet her. She was wearing a pair of navy jeans, tight fitting with the lace in the back. Her blouse was also tight fitting and I think it was also navy blue. It's hard to distinguish colors when you see a figure like Helen's.

I think she had shoes on, too. I knew I had to meet this girl, so I got up and stepped up to the juke-box right next to her. Her head came to about my shoulder, I had to look down when I spoke. I was ready for her, she was going to get the Dekker, you can't be turned down, double whammy, a can't miss approach. My best.

"Hi," I said. "Number nine's a nice tune."

She glanced down at the selections. "Number nine, what's the name of that one?"

"I don't know, I just picked that one out so's I could talk to you." She was much prettier than the paper I'd been reading.

"My name's Johnny," I blurted out.

"I know."

"You know . . . What else do you know?"

"I know you wanted to meet me. I know I wanted to meet you. But only I had the courage to make it happen."

Just like that, she knocked the whammy back two hundred years.

I turned to Vi in the booth. "You son of a gun."

She smiled up at me and sang, "You got a tiger by the tail, Johnny Dekker!"

I liked that, especially the tail part. I was in love.

When Helen left the grill that night she was on my arm.

She lived with her parents on Wallace Avenue, a ten minute walk from the grill. We arrived at her folk's home forty-five minutes later. It was a beautiful fall night with a little chill in the air, but we did not notice it. I was about to follow her up the steps to her front door, but she hesitated for a moment, took my hand and led me down the narrow walkway between the houses and to the back yard. She walked to the garage, took a key from out of her purse and opened the door. She beckoned me to follow. I followed.

"Have you got a match, Johnny? I don't want daddy to see the light go on."

I produced a match and brought it to life. She took a candle from a shelf and held the wick over the match flame. The candle flame cast eerie shadows upon the walls of the garage. In the center of the garage, with its wheels on blocks of wood, was a vintage car. I walked over to it, then I walked around it with Helen in my wake. It was hard to see by candlelight, but it looked like it was in excellent condition. I walked around the front and read the name above the radiator. It was a Hup-mobile, probably 1924 or 1925. Four doors with a trunk on the back and a wheel imbedded in both front fenders. What I would have given for that car, a real classic.

Helen opened the back door, got in and blew the candle out. "Get in here, silly, it's cold out there."

I swear, I thought I had broken my shin-bone on the running board in my rush to get into that car. "Damn it!" I cried.

Helen pulled me toward her. "What's the matter?"

I rubbed my shin bone. "I hurt my leg getting into this box car." Man, was this a big seat, I thought.

She put her hand on my leg and began to gently rub it. "Does this feel better?"

Our lips met and she kept rubbing ever so gently. Her lips were moist and had the taste of mint. We held each other in a long embrace. I always thought of myself as a person who could get into or out of any situation, but Helen was too much for me.

Suddenly, the lights went on and the garage burst into brightness. I untangled myself from Helen and looked through the front windshield of the car. I didn't feel the hurt in my shin-bone. I only felt I had to get the hell out of there, and quick! I stepped out of the car slowly. I did not know what to expect. What I saw was a man dressed in a knee length raincoat with a hat that looked like something Sherlock Holmes had thrown away. He wore glasses and had a sharp, thin nose. Who was this guy?

Helen rushed past me cursing, "Fredie, you sneaky bastard." At the same time her foot came up and caught him squarely in the jewelry department. What a shot. I reminded myself to call up the Chicago Bears. Helen would make one hell of a field goal kicker. Within seconds, Helen was out the door. Before following her, I glanced down at Fredie. He was on both knees, sweat covered his forehead and he kept rocking his head up and down. His system was telling him, "either throw up or crap, but do something!"

A whimper escaped his lips. I could not help myself. I felt sorry for him, he was in great pain. He looked up at me, asking for help with his eyes. I wanted to show him pity. He sensed this and I gave him an encouraging smile.

"Nice stop, Fredie," I said walking out the door.

Helen was standing in the gangway next to the house. I walked to her and she took me in her arms, squeezing me close to her.

"Tomorrow, Johnny, I'll see you tomorrow." Her hand was on my leg again and moved slowly, tantalizing me. I'll tell you one thing, this was a hell of a lot better than getting drop-kicked.

On the way to 718 I stopped at the paper stand, it was closed.

What a night, talk about luck! Arriving at 718, I was greeted by my cohorts and their women. Dugan must have seen the disappointment in my face.

"Didn't score, huh?" And he went back to reading the want ads.

"I don't believe it." Vi exclaimed. "Impossible."

"You don't know John," Bob said.

"But we know Helen," Kay Kay and Vi said, breaking into laughter. "She's the hottest thing that ever squatted between a pair of cowboy boots."

I let them have their fun and then told them the story of Fredie. And then Vi told me the story of Fredie. And I wondered why Helen hadn't told me the story about Fredie. And now, I was pissed off. Fredie, it seems had been going with Helen for over a year and could not quite keep up with Helen in the love department. At first, it had been the hottest relationship in West Pullman. Vi swore Helen and Fredie made love five or six times a night, they really rocked that old Hupmobile, according to Vi. But then, like anything else, the honeymoon was over. Fredie was running out of steam and Helen went out looking for someone that could stay with her in the saddle. John Dekker was that someone. Well, she wasn't going to make me her new stud, not me, pal. I got class.

That night it seemed like she would never show up, every five minutes I was looking up at the clock. She finally arrived and I was completely shocked; her face was covered with bruises and her left eye was almost closed. She sat next to me in the booth and placed her head on my shoulder. I pulled her close to me.

"Fredie?" I asked softly.

Her answer was slow in coming. I held her, trembles came from deep within her; her sobs were soft, profound. "Oh, Johnny, it was my dad." It was a confession and humiliation all at the same time. I waited for the sobs to subside. When she had gathered her composure, I got up.

"Let's get out of here." It was a request, not an order.

I can imagine how embarrassed she was walking up to the cash register. I wanted to knock some heads together. It's human nature to look at a person, but the people in the grill were staring and I was very uncomfortable. I did nothing, I just smiled back and gave them the finger. It was amazing how so many people could turn their heads at the same time and go back to eating their hamburgers and fries. Sheik was at the register and took our check. He said nothing about the incident and avoided looking at Helen. Sheik had class written all over him. Regardless of his pleasures and the life style he chose, I would always respect him for what he said:

"John, that's your name, isn't it?"

"Yeah."

"I don't know what went down with the little lady, but if you come up with any problems, you see me, huh?"

I took his hand. It was soft, but his grip was firm.

"Appreciate that, Sheik, thanks!"

"Say, hello, to Bob for me. I'd appreciate that."

"I'll do that, Sheik. But, I'm afraid Bob's all tied up. His girl has one baking in the oven and he's so worried about it that he's thinking of getting a regular job."

"Oh?"

"Dugan's available, though."

"So are the apes at Brookfield Zoo." Sheik almost laughed aloud.

"Yeah, and they got more hair than Dugan." This time he laughed.

"See ya," Helen was waiting for me on the sidewalk.

"What was that all about?" she asked.

Just like a woman. There she was, face black and blue, shivering from the cold, her whole world turned inside out, and she asks, "What was that all about?"

"Never mind what that was all about. Right now I want to find out what this is all about." I took her hand before she could answer and started across the street. I knew what she was going to ask me, so I beat her to it. "We're going to 718, you can explain it to me there."

Bob met us at the door, gave Helen a cheery hello, glanced at her face and quickly turned to me. His eyes showed concern, but he was at a loss for words. He looked to Helen and then back to me.

36

"Rough day, huh?"

Dugan was reading the want ads again. Vi and Kay were debating on what to call the baby. When they saw Helen they each gave me a look that would kill. "What happened to you, honey?" They sounded like the Gold Dust Twins. Their eyes fell on me again. "Did you . . . ?"

Isn't that the way it always is? If I had brought a dog home with a broken leg, they would have accused me of running him over with my car. Hell, I don't even own a car, but, if I did, I'd run them over. I loved these gals, but I sure wouldn't want them on my jury. I took Helen over to the couch and we sat down before I answered them. "Helen, tell these people what happened before they hang me."

Dugan looked up from his paper for the first time, checked out the bruises on Helen's face and threw the paper down on the floor. "Who did this, kid? Tell me, and I'll kill the bum for you!"

"Can't kill this guy," I said.

"Okay, so we break his legs." Dugan was cooling down.

"Maybe one," I joked. I hoped this chit-chat with Dugan was calming Helen down and it seemed to be working. It appeared she had gathered her composure together and began talking to Vi and Kay Kay. I got up from the couch and walked over to Dugan and Bob. On the way to the table I picked up Dugan's paper. I winked at Dugan and said softly, so only he could hear. "Maybe two, Buddie?"

"What's the poop, John?" Bob's curiosity got the best of him. "Who's legs we gunna break?"

"Daddy's!" Helen broke in suddenly. "My stinking old man tried to rape me last night!"

"I'll cut his nose off!" Dugan bellowed. "And, I'll shove it in his ear!"

"It will just about fit there." Helen managed a smile and I admired her, this gal had guts. She had almost been raped, she had the hell beat out of her and she took it like a champion.

The story she told us was pathetic. After leaving me the night before she went into the house through the back door and went to her room. The room had been dark, and as she closed the door behind her, she heard a strange sound. She hit the light switch and discovered her father sitting on the bed. He motioned for her to sit down beside him. This had happened three or four times in the past and she was not alarmed, because in the past nothing had occurred. They had just sat there and talked, he held her gently in his arms. He wept openly of how much he missed her mother. How, since the death of his wife, he had been so lonely. He had held Helen but never tried fondling her, until last night . . .

"Was he drinking?" I asked.

"Makes no difference," Dugan said.

"No, he wasn't drinking." Helen went on. "That chintzy son-of-a-bitch never paid for a drink in his life. He's still got the first nickel he ever made, and, what he rakes in on the horses in the steel mill, that's a bundle, too."

"Your ol' man's a bookie?" I asked.

"He's not a bookie, he IS the bookie in the shops."

If you could have looked into Bob's, Dugan's and my head, you would have seen dollar signs. We all wanted to ask the same question. But did not know how. Helen answered it for us, I just had to put a thought in her mind.

"Helen, you want to get even with that creep?" She nodded and I continued. "We'll drop a dime on him, we'll call the I.R.S. They'll check his bank account out, and bingo, pop's goes to the shit house for about ten years."

"That wouldn't do any good, Johnny. Daddy don't trust banks, he hides his money in the house."

I was never so happy in all my life, but I tried to appear deected. "Never mind, honey, we'll get him some other way."

I wanted to change the subject, but Dugan beat me to it.

"Vi, get Helen some blankets. She's staying with us for a while."

Helen slept with me on the couch that night. It was kind of crowded, but we didn't mind. We finally fell to sleep around 2:00 a.m. I think we set a new world's record for something.

*Chapter 6*

## *"Wheels Are Turning"*

It felt like I didn't sleep all night, but, yet, I was up by the time Vi had a pot of coffee brewed. "What time is it?" I asked, rubbing the cobwebs from my eyes.

She turned from the stove and giggled, "After the night you had, how could you be up this early? I swear I heard Helen groaning half the night and I know it wasn't from that mouse she's got under her eye."

Dugan's head appeared from under the covers. "Vi, tell the guy what time it is, will ya? And John, drink your coffee, okay?" He pulled the covers back over his head and I heard him mumbling something about not getting enough sleep.

I whispered to Vi, "What time is it?"

"Eight o'clock," she whispered back.

"Eight o'clock!" I shouted. "God, it's eight o'clock, Dugan. I'll see you later."

Dugan came flying up from under the covers and stood up on the bed, he was completely naked. "Give me my pants, I'm gunna kill that wise guy!" Then he smiled and placed his hands over his crotch. "Gee, it's cold in here. Where the hell are you going in the middle of the night, anyway?"

I drank my coffee down in a gulp. It was chilly outside, so I put on my light jacket. When I reached the door I answered him. "We need a car, I'm going to buy one. I'll explain later. Get some food together. I'll be back about twelve, we'll go to the park and have a picnic."

"It might be snowing by then."

"Then we'll go ice skating. Just get the food together. I'll see you later."

Stepping out the door I was greeted by a brisk, fall morning. I flipped up the collar on my jacket and started hoofing it to my folks' home. There were a few people out on the street, some walking their dog, others either going to work or returning from work. There was a dusting of frost on the car windows and the trees were turning from pool table green to bright yellow, browns and reds. The air was clear and the sun promised a warmer afternoon.

My folks lived about a mile from 718. I decided to make a pit stop at the Normal Grill for a second cup of coffee. Sheik was behind the counter working the grill. There was one waitress working the booths and she was kept busy serving the ham and eggers.

I straddled a seat at the counter, looked up and down, my eye caught who I guessed was Fredie. It had to be him. No two people in the world would own a hat like that. He gave me a casual glance and continued to read the menu. It was apparent he did not recognize me or chose not to. It would have been nice if I could have seen him walk.

If it was Fredie, he'd be walking real funny. I didn't let it bother me. I knew Fredie and I were going to have a talk down the line anyway, so I let it slide.

"What will it be, Johnny?" Sheik asked, drying his hands on his apron.

"You still got that three-egg special?"

"Sure, how do you want your eggs?"

I could not help myself. I always wanted to use this one. "I want one scrambled, one boiled and one over easy."

"Okay." He turned to the grill and hummed to himself. From that moment on I made up my mind I wouldn't try and out maneuver this gentleman. Damn it, I don't even like boiled eggs.

The breakfast was good and filled an empty spot in my stomach. I was ready for the day ahead. I had one more cup of coffee, took my check and a ten dollar bill and handed it to Sheik. "Great breakfast, Sheik. The boiled egg was a little too hard, so I left it on the plate."

Sheik had a devilish grin on his face. "You didn't try that egg, John. If you did, you would have found out it was raw."

I took the change he gave me and gave him a hurt look. "You spoiled my day, Sheik, you know that?"

"It's early yet." he laughed.

He wouldn't find it so funny when he found that ten cent tip I left under my plate. Wrong. Knowing the Sheik, he'd laugh.

Mom was in the kitchen when I got there. Her glasses were down on the tip of her nose, she was reading her horoscope. She looked up, surprised at seeing me. I had not been home in over a month, but I had checked in almost every night over the phone. If I hadn't, I would have had hell to pay.

"Johnny!" she said, she appeared excited. "Don't go out today. Your horoscope says you will find gainful employment."

"Mom, can I hide in the basement?"

We both hugged and kissed each other, gossiped about everyone in the neighborhood, hugged and kissed some more and then I had to leave. I promised to return the follow Sunday for dinner.

"I'll be waiting," she said half-heartedly.

"I'll be here, you can bet on it, Ma."

"Sure . . ."

"I'll be here. Bye, now."

My next stop was the basement. It was here I kept my stash. The coffee can was hidden behind some old canning jars my mother had stacked on the back shelf. The jars had been there since my grandpa and grandma passed away. And, my mother, not in a million years, would ever use these jars, not while they had grocery stores, anyway. I took the money out and tossed the can over in the corner. I counted the money, there was still three hundred and seventeen dollars left over from my bookie enterprise.

I figured the best place to look for a used car would be in the local newspaper. So I walked to the corner drug store and picked one up. As my finger went down the used car column, it hesitated. There was the car I wanted; 1932 Buick four-door, $300.00, runs great, beautiful black finish.

I went into the drug store and called the number in the paper. A lady answered. I asked if she still had the car. She said, she did. I asked her when I could see it and she told me any time I wanted to. She gave me her address. That was a problem, her home was at least three miles away and I did not feel like walking there. If I did not like the car it would be a wasted effort.

"Mam," I asked, "is there any chance you could drive the car over to 119th and Wentworth? I'm in a drugstore here and I have no way to get to your house. Do you think you can do that, Mam?"

"119th and Wentworth? Sure, I'll leave right away. I'll be there in about ten minutes. I know where the store is, and it's no problem."

"Thank you, mam. I'll be waiting outside. I'm wearing a light blue jacket and blue pants, you won't miss me."

"Okay, then, I'll see you shortly." and she hung up.

She was there in ten minutes. I must have caught her between hair-curlers and make up. She apologized for the way she looked and we quickly got down to business. I drove the car around the block a few times and must have scared the hell out of her pulling away from the curb. The clutch wasn't as smooth as my dad's Ford. I stalled and jerked for the first hundred feet. I tested the brakes and steering, they seemed to be all right.

"You got a deal, mam. I'll take the car. But, you'll have to take me home to get the money. It'll only take a few minutes."

She agreed. I asked her to drive to 718. We were not going for money, we were going to get Bob. He had a driver's license and I didn't.

We arrived at 718 within ten minutes. Everyone was dressed and ready for the picnic. I told them it would have to be delayed until we got the car business taken care of. Bob drove the woman back to her house, paid her the three hun-

42

dred I had given him, got the title for the car and was back at 718 before I had my second cup of coffee.

"How'd it handle?" I asked, as he came into the apartment.

"Great," he answered. "Needs a grease job and probably an oil change, and I think one headlight is burned out. Maybe, it's a fuse, I don't know, but, other than that, you got a nice car."

"Think it will hold that picnic lunch?" I laughed, pointing to a large wicker basket.

Dugan took Vi's hand. "We worked up an appetite last night, and that yum yum basket looks great."

We were all in a good mood, even Helen got into the act. "Has it got a large seat, Johnny?" she giggled. "You know how I like a lot of comfort."

She had cleaned herself up pretty good. Vi and Kay Kay had managed to conceal the mouse Helen had under her eye with make-up, and the ice packs she had put on the night before had reduced the swelling to where it was hardly noticeable. But, the hurt was still there, and *daddy* was going to pay for it, in spades . . . .

"It's got a big seat, but so have you." I joked slapping her across the butt. "Now, let's get on with the picnic."

At the park I managed to get Dugan and Bob away from the girls and we discussed Helen's father. The way it looked, we had a good score going here, and in no way were we going to mess it up by being in a hurry. This had to be done right, and, if it was all right with them, I'd figure it out. There would be no mistakes. We'd do it right or we wouldn't do it at all.

"Do you agree?" I asked.

"You run it, John." Bob said.

"Ditto," Dugan echoed.

"Give me a week, guys. I'll pump Helen, and then we'll nail this guy."

The picnic went well. We stayed at the park the better part of the afternoon. The girls played the guys in a game of baseball, it was a pitcher's duel—girls 23, boys, 21—and we were all exhausted when we arrived at 718. After the long day, I was hoping Helen would fall right to sleep.

She didn't . . .

Recreating the events that occurred between Helen and me that evening, I feel it would only be detrimental to the well being of my reader. Therefore, I will omit any reference to it, except to say, "My God! She's trying to kill me!"

*Chapter 7*

## "The Fix"

Bob and I were out of the apartment well before eight o'clock and on our way to the D.M.V. I had to get the title changed over into my name, apply for plates and get a driver's license. I calculated this chore would take most of the day and we'd be lucky if we got home in time for supper. I figured wrong, it was my good fortune to get into a line that was not only short, but the clerk at the filing desk was the father of an ex-school mate of mine.

"Good morning, Mr. Panozzo. Nice seeing you again," I said in greeting.

"And a good morning to you, sir." he replied. "And how may I help you?"

"My name's John Dekker, Mr. Panozzo, and I'm a friend of your son, Victor." I saw recognition in his face. "I need to get this paper work done."

"You know Victoro and my other son, Raymond?"

"Sure. Ray and me went to Scanlan together. Vic was two grades ahead of me, but we ran around together all the time. How are your sons, anyway?"

"Raymond, he's still home with me, but Victoro . . ." A far away look entered his eyes. "Victoro, he's in the Marine Corps., somewhere in the Pacific called Iwo Jima."

His hand was on the counter and I took it in mine. "Don't worry, Mr. Panozzo. Vic will be okay, he's as tough as they come and he can take care of himself. I know, he's kicked my butt a dozen times."

We both laughed and he shook my hand with genuine friendship.

"Okay, kid, what have we got here?" He said, taking the papers

I had placed on the counter. "Ah huh, that's right. Plates, title and driver's license. Yes, everything's in order. You've got the car out there, have you?"

"Yes."

He leaned over the counter, made sure no one was watching and said, "When you go outside to take your test, you see a long string-bean fella. His name's Marco. You tell him I sent you. He will give you the test. After the test, drop a ten dollar bill on the seat, he'll take care of the rest. Capisce?"

"I got it, and thanks, Mr. Panozzo."

I started to leave the counter but he called me back. "Hey, John, your mama, she reads cards?"

"Yeah."

"She's full of bullshit, you know that?"

"Yeah, I know it, but I love her."

"Everybody does, she's a fine woman."

"Thanks, Mr. Panozzo. And don't worry about Vic, that dago can kick the Jap's ass all by himself."

"You're full of bullshit, too."

"That's no bullshit, Mr. Panozzo."

Taking the papers in hand, I walked outside and found Marco right away. He was a string-bean, all right. He stood at least six foot six and weighed approximately one hundred and forty pounds. I gave him the papers and mentioned Mr. Panozzo. Twenty minutes later and ten dollars lighter I had a temporary driver's license, plates for the car and no lectures. Ten dollars well spent.

We arrived back at the apartment at ten thirty. Dugan walked out to the curb and met us.

"Greetings." He poked his head through the open window on the passenger's side. "You get the paper work done?"

"No sweat, the guy said I was the best driver he ever saw."

"What guy?"

"Mr. Hamilton, the guy on the ten dollar bill."

Dugan smiled. "Always the wise guy, huh, John?"

"Not always. I'm still not sure what we're going to do about Helen. We don't want her staying here. That would put heat on us after we pull the caper. Right now, nobody knows she's staying here or going with me and we want to keep it that way. We'll have to find a place for her to stay. You got any suggestions?"

Dugan and Bob both shook their heads in the negative. I thought the matter over. She could not go home. We did not have enough money to put her up in an apartment and I sure was not going to stay with her at 718. That would put heat on the caper, and above all, it would put extreme heat on my body. I decided to see the Sheik, between him and I, we would come up with an answer. I would see him that afternoon when he wasn't too busy. In the meantime, we would play with our new toy. I asked the girls to get a bucket of soapy water and some rags, and we all pitched in cleaning up the Buick.

We knocked off at around noon and enjoyed potato salad and sandwiches Vi had made. Dugan was lucky, Vi was one hell of a cook. Bob had a spoiled brat and I had a love machine. Relief was coming through. I knew Sheik would come up with something. He had to or I was certain to reach an early death.

I did not approach Helen on the subject of her dad's house, I had enough problems in trying to find her a place to stay. I had mixed feelings about Helen. I cared for her, but it was not love, or maybe it was just too much love on her part. I needed space and Helen would not provide it. I knew in my heart that this affair would not last, because I knew me. I was not the settling down type, not yet, anyway. I had places to see, things to do, and I didn't intend to have a Helen on my arm. I had to figure a way to break off with her after the caper, and I had to do it right. It would have to appear as though she was doing the breaking off, because, as they say, "Hell hath no fury, like a woman scorned." I had no idea how this was all to come about, but it would.

After lunch, I jumped into the Buick and headed for the Normal Grill. I went alone because after I talked with Sheik, I was going to run over to my folks' house and show the car to dad. I knew he would look it over from hood to trunk and then give me his opinion in his most professional fashion.

Sheik was glad to see me (maybe, he expected another dime). I told him I had a little problem and he motioned me to a booth. As I had anticipated, business was slow. He spoke to the waitress and took the seat across from me.

"What's up?' he asked.

I ran it down to him in the simplest of terms, but did not mention the burglary. I tried to impress upon him that I was merely doing this until I had the funds to get her an apartment of her own.

"You need money then?" His eyes met mine and held them. "John, don't con me. You don't buy a car in the morning and then go out hustling rent money in the afternoon. I'll help you. There's no problem, but you level with me or get the hell out of here."

I did what I had to do. I walked out.

Before I reached the car he was at my side.

"Okay, John, she moves in with me tomorrow. She's safe with me, you know that. And John . . . ."

"What?"

"Did anyone ever tell you that you had a temper?'

"To answer question number one, yes, I know she's safe with you, and two, yes, I've got a temper. There's two more things; are you safe with her? And she moves in tonight. Tomorrow may be too late."

I thought for a moment my joke went right over his head, but he turned at the door of the grill and said "Dekker, you are nuts."

"Sheik, you don't know how nuts." I left him with that thought in mind. It could mean anything and I liked to play mind games. Sheik would make a good opponent.

I didn't have to go into the house to get my father out to see the car. I wasn't even out of the car and he came hustling down the sidewalk. My mother, Toots and Billy were in his wake. Like follow the leader, they circled the car behind my father. I knew what was in my mother's mind. She was thinking, where did Johnny steal the money? Or, did Johnny steal the car? I always knew when the worry bug hit my mother, she had this habit of giggling when there was something on her mind that bothered her.

"Nice car, Jonathan." That Jonathan was a tip off, too.

"Mom, it's bought and paid for," I soothed her. "I won the money in a dice game last night."

"It's nice, but it's a G.M.C. product," my dad cut in. "What did you pay for it?"

"Three bills. Some old lady was driving it. It runs like a dream."

"Ford runs like a dream. Your car is missing. I heard it as you drove up. Probably needs plugs and points." Dad pushed out his hand. "Give me the keys, John. I'll take it around the block and check it out."

While he was out testing the car, Mom, Toots, Billy and I went into the house. On the stove was a boiling pot of water, it was just about ready to erupt its contents of hot dogs. In the smoking oven was a pan of macaroni. It resembled a bed of molten lava going down the sides of the pan. She just shook her head, took the pan out of the oven with a pot holder and threw the smoking mess into the sink. She went to the pantry, took two large cans from the shelf and opened them.

"Hot dogs and beans, anyone?"

"I was thinking of macaroni, Ma."

"Shut up, Jonathan."

She was still thinking, but now she was mad and thinking.

Fortunately, dad walked into the house, otherwise, Jonathan and Madam Dekker were heading for a showdown, and damn it, I never win. One thing about my mother, you could not con her. The only way I could even get a draw off of her, was to use reverse psychology. Tell her the truth. This left her so frustrated she would go to the clothes closet, retrieve the bottle of wine she had hidden there (wine, she thought we didn't know about) and take a belt or two. Thanks to dad appearing on the scene this ritual was avoided.

"Bring it around tomorrow, John. We'll give it a tune-up and adjust the clutch. For a G.M.C., it runs pretty good. Not quite the pickup of a Ford, though." He washed and dried his hands and turned to my mother. "I'm ready for that macaroni now, dear."

I wasn't sure, but I think she was heading for the closet.

After supper, I hung around and played monopoly for an hour or two with Toots and Billy. When I left, I was bankrupt and in jail, all my property and money had been stolen by my unscrupulous little brother.

I returned to 718 around nine thirty. Dugan and Vi had gone to a movie with Bob and Kay Kay. I was alone with Helen! Monopoly, and now this. She was sitting, legs crossed, on the sofa combing her hair. The lighting was low, but I could see she was fully dressed and I let out a sigh of relief. "Hi," I said sitting down beside her.

I could see she had been crying. "Hi, Johnny," she sniffed.

"What's wrong, something bothering you?"

"Yes."

"Well, what is it? Whatever it is, we can fix it."

"Oh, it's just something Dugan said."

"What, what?"

"He said it was too crowded around here and I would have to move. Where can I go, Johnny? I have no money, I have nothing but the clothes on my back, and I'm sure not going to move back home. I'd rather sleep on the street than be with that bastard."

I put my arm around her shoulder and gave her a gentle pat. Things were going to work out all right. I turned her toward me and kissed her on the nose. She raised her head a fraction and our lips met. I had to keep my wits about me, I like sex, but Helen would try to make an all-night session out of this and we had to visit the Sheik.

"Give me your brush. I'll do the back for you."

"It's done already, you big dope, can't you see?"

I had her attention off of sex. "About Dugan," I began. "This is his pad and he says who goes and who stays. It's nothing personal, he even asked me to find my own place a week ago. Then he realized I was paying the rent, and he hasn't mentioned it since, but he's right, it is crowded around here, so the only problem is we have to find you a place to stay. That way we can have more time to ourselves and not worry about someone walking across our bed in the middle of the night. Hang on a minute, I've got an idea. I have to make a phone call."

I called Sheik up and made arrangements to drop Helen off at the grill around one a.m. He said the after movie crowd would be gone by then. That was great, but what the hell was I going to do for the next three hours? What was I going to do. I was going to pump Helen about her father's house, that's what I was going to do.

I returned to the sofa, she looked at me with those soft, brown eyes. Pump her, not hump her, I said to myself. "It's all fixed, you have nothing to worry about, Helen. I just called Sheik and made arrangements for you to stay at his apartment until I rustle up enough money to get us a place of our own. We meet him at one o'clock."

For the first time that night a smile came to her face. I can imagine the thoughts that had gone through her head before I told her about Sheik. It's a terrible feeling not to know what the next moment will bring you. "Oh, that's wonderful!" You could feel it in her voice, that a great burden had been lifted. "I like Sheik."

Was she in for a surprise.

"There's something I wanted to talk to you about, Helen. But, I don't know exactly how to start. We're going to have to get some money so we can get ourselves a nice place. So, I was wondering, ah . . ."

"So you were wondering how we could rob my father, right?"

"Helen, take your clothes off."

*Chapter 8*

## "Show Time"

The next two weeks went well, things were beginning to fall into place; Helen was shaping up in more ways than one, she was happy living with the Sheik, but more than this, she was less possessive and very excited about the burglary. I pretended like the burglary was an old, everyday thing to me, and I guess I sounded like it, because she said I sounded so professional. Sure, I was the greatest burglar since Captain Kangaroo. I toss milk cases through windows. I didn't mention that to Helen though. Stan's was sure a not pro job, it's a wonder I didn't cut my head off going through his glass door. I had only talked to her twice since she had moved in with the Sheik, it was always strictly business and, to my surprise, we put sex completely out of the picture. This was strange and it crossed my mind for a fleeting moment, perhaps, maybe, Helen was playing games with one of the Sheik's boy friends. Was I jealous? On the contrary. If this was the case, I would become indignant, hurt, oh, yes, hurt. But I would forgive her, I would understand, and I would get the hell out of her life as fast as I could. But this was just fantasy, I could never be that lucky.

While Helen stayed with Sheik, I stayed with my mother and father.

It would not serve our cause for me to remain with Dugan and the gang. As of now, nobody was aware that we hung out together and I hoped to keep it that way. Dugan was a little sad to see me go, but I understood that: the rent was due. I didn't have two pennies to rub together so I couldn't help him. But I had a plan and I put it into motion. I went to see Sheik, explained the situation and offered him the title of my car for

52

a one hundred dollar loan. He gave me the hundred and told me to keep the title. 69;Just don't forget where you got the hundred, John," he said. "That's a lot of hamburgers."

I met Dugan and Bob twice that week; we met in the same park we had played ball in and we discussed the burglary.

"Any suggestions?" I asked them.

"We told you, you run it, John, so run it." Dugan spoke for the both of them.

They listened attentively as I laid out the plan. We were going to make this burglary look like the work of some real pro's. From the information I had gathered, Helen's father worked as a foreman in the steel mill. His hours were from eight in the morning until three-thirty in the afternoon. He left the mill at three-thirty, caught the Riverdale street car and was home at approximately four-thirty every evening. He never stopped for a drink or anything else. It was get on the street car, get off the street car, and go home. Same routine every day. I followed him to work in the morning and I was waiting for him when he left at night. I did this three times and it was just like Helen had said, no variations. Pa Pa was like a robot. The more she told me, the sicker I got. This deal could not be pulled off in broad daylight. It would not only be risky, it would be insane. When I explained this to Dugan and Bob, it was evident they were becoming sick, also. Dugan broke into the conversation one time, "Screw 'em, I'll go through the front door, *sap** the guy, tie him up and you guys get the loot."

I had been waiting for him to come on with something like that, so now I could break the good news to him. I just wanted to see him squirm a little.

Helen had told me that, since her mother's death, her father had not been dating other women. The only time he ventured out was at night on Saturday. He either took in a movie or went to play poker at the pool room. He would usually return home around eleven o'clock. I watched him for two Saturdays in a row. That's exactly what he did. I played pool with

* *Sap: Blunt instrument to render a person unconscious.*

my Uncle Fred and watched our *mark* stroll out of the pool room around eleven. He was a short man in his late fifties and, from what I saw and heard, a very argumentative sort. He played poker loosely and expected to win every hand. When he lost he complained to everyone in the place. I recognized him as a born loser.

The guys were all smiles when I told them of the poker game, and I have to admit, it was going to be a setup. We would pull the job the next Saturday night. The weather had grown colder and this was good, because people tend to close their windows when it gets cold and the chances were excellent nobody would hear us. The way I had it figured, Dugan and Bob would pull the burglary while I played poker with Helen's old man. I wanted it to go this way for two reasons: one, if the old man left the poker game early, I would call Dugan up immediately and tell him to blow the scene, and two, I had the perfect alibi, I was playing poker with Pa Pa. I fully expected to get picked up for the burglary. There was no question in my mind about that. People knew I had been seeing Helen, and people would be questioned. Fredie for one. Pa Pa knew she had been seeing Fredie. Pa Pa would tell the police about Fredie; Fredie would be picked up and tell them about Johnny. Johnny would be picked up and give the fuzz his alibi. Coincidence, yes, but you can't convict a man on coincidence. I'd be locked up for a day, then they either turned me loose or I'd get a lawyer.

Dugan and Bob went along whole heartedly with my plan. They did not complain or even suggest that I had the easy part of the caper, which in fact, I didn't. There was a good chance I would go to jail and a better chance I would get knocked around. Chicago Cops had a habit of doing things like that, especially, if you are a wise guy, and I, at times, can be a wise guy. My problem now was Dugan, this mad man had to be controlled. In no way was he to blow the whole show on some stupid maneuver, like losing his cool if things didn't go exactly to his liking. I repeated over and over, just go according to the plan, no variations. If everything fell into place, the caper would go off without a hitch. By watching the old man on Saturday night, I knew he would be in the poker game between seven and eight p.m., he was covered. I would be in the pool room awaiting his arrival. When he got there, I'd call Dugan at 718; within five minutes, Dugan and Bob would be on their way. Nothing would go wrong, one hour tops, and they should be in and out. They would have no trouble getting into the joint; Helen had given me the keys to the back door. It was like we owned the place.

Dugan would enter the back door with Bob, lock it behind them and make their search. They would use pillow cases to carry the loot, nothing large was to be taken, just money and jewels; no silverware or anything bulky. They would then exit the same way they entered and go to the basement window in the back yard. Bob would go and pick up the work car. In the meantime, Dugan would break the window with a jimmy bar and tear up the sliding bolt lock on the window. We sure didn't want the cops to know we had keys, did we? Dugan's chore would not take over a minute. Bob would be waiting for him in the alley and they'd be on their way to 718. Me, I was going to enjoy the poker game. I had no intentions on leaving the game until Pa Pa went home, and then I would stay for an hour longer. It was great, the old man would be my alibi along with six other guys in the poker game.

Helen and I were with each other most of Saturday morning. My last instructions to her were, "You hang around the Normal Grill tonight between eight and ten. Try to have someone with you. Fredie would be great if you can arrange it."

"I can arrange it."

I had to give her credit. She didn't appear nervous at all. Me, I had apprehensions, not about being caught, that didn't enter my mind. The caper would go down fine, it was afterward that bothered me. If I got picked up by the law, I'd hold down my end as I'm sure Bob and Dugan would have done the same. But, the hassle of going through bails, lawyers, court rooms and all that other crap didn't appeal to me. We'd beat any case they had against us, but that takes months, sometimes years. In order to avoid this unpleasantness, I suggested to Dugan and Bob, that after the caper they get lost for a few weeks. Bob could go to Iowa and show Kay Kay the fall corn harvest and, at the same time, tell Bob's mother she was going to be a grandmother. Dugan was another matter. He was a city boy, so I suggested he and Vi go to the Big Apple, take in the Statue of Liberty, bet a few horses, see a few shows and come home in about three weeks. I would stay home, live with my folks and pretend I'm broke. If I had to, I'd even find a job.

The day went fast and at six o'clock I planned on being at the pool room. Dugan, Bob and I were going over last minute details. In two hours, it was show time!

"If the old man leaves early," I told Dugan, "I'll call you at Helen's house. You'll know it's me, because I'll ask you right away, 'What's playing at the movie tonight?' If you don't hear that, then tell the caller they got the wrong number. I don't expect Papa to leave early, but if he does, you'll have plenty of time to get out of there."

"We got it," they said together.

"Okay, stay here till I call. I'm on my way."

It was exactly six when I arrived at the pool room. I looked around for Helen's father. Not seeing him, I strolled to the back and checked out the poker table. The game had started early and there were four players, all regulars. Black Sam, the owner of the pool room, was just sitting in the game until the table filled up. When the table was full, he would get up for another player and start collecting his 5% off of every pot. I decided to hold off for the time being. I was just holding forty dollars on me and I had to make it last me the night. There was no sense of taking a chance of losing the money before Helen's father showed up. I'd look pretty silly just standing there all night.

I walked over to the wall and took down a cue stick down, set the balls up on the table and practiced my shots, which were none. Uncle Fred had tried a number of times to get me to play pool, no betting, he'd never take my money, but just to relax and enjoy the game. I was relaxing now and it only cost me a quarter a game.

At seven-fifteen Helen's father walked in and took a seat at the poker table. At seven-twenty, I called Dugan at 718.

"You're on," I said, when he answered the phone. "He's playing now."

"Right, John. I'll see you at the house later."

I walked directly back to the poker table and took a seat across from the old man. I didn't want to get shut out or I'd have to wait half the night to get a seat.

"Give me forty worth of chips," I asked Sam. "Tonight's my night."

Little did he know what I was thinking of. It sure wasn't poker and if I wasn't careful, I'd lose my shirt. Poker is a game of concentration, luck and skill. I had luck, very little skill and no concentration. With these as my tools I managed to milk my forty dollars until the old man got up and called it a night. He was on schedule, it was ten to eleven. I waited and played until midnight before I cashed in my chips. To my surprise, I was only six dollars out.

"See you guys," I said to the players. "Don't spend my six bucks all in one place."

"Stop by anytime, kid," Sam said. "We play every Saturday night."

"I'll do that."

*Chapter 9*

# "The Split"

My size ten shoes covered a lot of ground in a very short time, returning to 718. I'd have to give up cigarettes, I was puffing like a full-back that had just run a hundred yards and had the play called back. I felt a great deal better when I spotted the Buick in front of 718. It had been a hectic night, I know my role in the caper was a minor one, but if you had any idea what went through my mind, you would not think so. I'd much rather be in on the score first hand. At least, when you're on the scene, you have no time to think of anything else but the business at hand. Seeing the Buick stopped my heart from pounding and a sense of relief passed over me.

I knocked on the door and Vi opened it for me with a smile on her face. It spelled success all over it.

"Johnny's here!" she yelled over her shoulder and then to me, "Where have you been? It's after twelve."

I walked into the room without answering her. Dugan, Bob and

Kay Kay were sitting crossed-legged, Indian style, in the center of the front room, each with a pile of money in front of them.

Dugan spoke first. "John, you won't believe this, but we got over twenty-three grand." He picked up a bundle of hundred dollar bills and waved them in the air. "I figure the total around thirty grand, and we ain't even counted the dollar bills."

"And we got a shoe box of gold watches, too," Bob burst in. "Some of them must be a hundred years old, and, look at this." He tossed me a leather bag with draw strings at the top.

I pulled the draw strings loose and shook some of the contents onto the palm of my hand, rings, a whole bag of rings. The three I had in my hand were diamond rings and my heart began to pound again. We had a fortune in the bag alone. Man, was there going to be heat after this caper.

I tried to be cool, professional, but I don't think it worked. "I guess we made a good score, huh, guys?"

"We did more than that, John. Wait till you hear this."

"Hear what, Dugan?"

"I had some fun, John."

"Oh boy! What-kind-of-fun, Dugan?" My words came very slow.

Dugan could not hold back. "Johnny, baby, that old creep was not only a bookie. He was a drug dealer! I found two plastic bags of heroin in his closet."

"Damn it, Dugan, you didn't nail that too?"

"John, I did what you would have done. I spread it all over the house, on all the rugs, in the closets and on the beds. It's all over the joint. It's gunna take the old man two weeks to clean up the mess I made. Man, there's no way in the world he can call the cops now."

What Dugan said was true, but what was the difference if he reported the burglary in two weeks or that day. There would be just as much heat and I would not have an alibi, because I would not know what day, or when he would report the burglary. Dugan had meant well, and the more I thought about it, the better I felt. The solution was simple; I'd go on a trip myself for about a month. Wherever I went, I would make sure people would notice me and that would be my alibi. The more I thought about it, the better it got. I would take my Uncle Fred with me. We would go to Miami and hang out in the pool halls. I'd give Uncle Fred enough money to hustle the local pool sharks. If he won, okay, if he lost, that was okay, too. This would work out fine. Dugan would be in New York, Bob would be picking corn and I would be in the sunny south for my birthday. To top it off, hallelujah, I'd be with Uncle Fred and not Helen.

I told the guys my plan and we finished counting out the money around two a.m. The total take came to thirty-one thousand and forty dollars. We split the money between the three of us and I put one thousand dollars aside for Helen. I suggested to Dugan and Bob to do the same for Vi and Kay Kay. That way there would be no bitching. There was one more thing to clear up and I pointed it out:

"I've got a deal I want to make with you guys." I said. "Let's bid on the watches and rings. We'll each mark down our top bid on a piece of paper. Top bidder gets it all, the other two guys split the bid money."

"You got a deal, John," Bob agreed.

"I'm for it, what the hell," Dugan echoed.

I asked Vi to get us three pieces of paper and three pens. Dugan stepped over to the side and marked down a figure. Bob turned his back, wrote down a number, scratched his head and turned around. We all walked to the kitchen table and placed each of our papers face down.

"Who's first?" I asked.

"I'll go first," Dugan volunteered. He turned the paper over. "Six hundred bucks."

Bob smiled and turned over his paper. "Nine hundred, pal."

"Pikers," I laughed, turning my paper over. "One thousand and one dollars, thank you."

I gave them each five one hundred dollar bills from off my stack, and asked, "You big spenders got change for a dollar?"

*Chapter 10*

## "A Letter From Dugan"

I stayed the rest of the night but left early in the morning. I had a lot of things to do. First, I'd have to see Uncle Fred and make arrangements for our trip. Then, I'd see Helen, give her the thousand and explain why I was leaving town. The rest of the day I would spend with my folks. I had no idea what I was going to tell my mother about this sudden trip, but I'd come up with something. Uncle Fred was delighted and it was no problem talking him into making our journey down south. Helen, to my surprise, did not put up an argument. It seems the night before, while in the company of Fredie, they had found a new meaning to their old love. Suddenly, it was once again in full bloom. Fredie was in, I was out. It was back to the newspaper for me, and somehow, I felt a little sad, like winning the lottery or something. Mom, on the other hand, was a little tougher. I came up with the story that Uncle Fred and I were going to Florida. Uncle Fred was going to foot the bill. She went for it, I think.

At least, I think she went for it . . . Perhaps, you would like to be the judge. Our conversation went something like this:

Mom: "Uncle Fred is going to pay all the expenses? Fred, my brother? Bull hockey."

Me: "He won the dough in a pool tournament, Ma."

Mom: "Sure, and Lindberg swam the Atlantic, too."

Me: "He did, Ma. He won five hundred bucks and he wants to go to Miami to hustle the pool halls. He wants to have me along in case they get wise to him."

Mom: "And what do you do if they get wise to him?"

Me: "I protect him. I keep them off of his back."

Mom: "Oh, that's nice. My little boy is going to protect my brother against a bunch of hoodlums in a pool hall a thousand miles away. And, what do you intend to protect him with, my son?"

Me: "Running shoes, Ma, and a number eighteen cue stick."

She went for it, right? I would appreciate your opinion, if you agree with me, please contact my publisher. Thank you.

### *"Off To Florida"*

On Monday morning I opened a safe deposit box in the Rumbell Real Estate and unloaded my goodies from the burglary. I had a little over eight thousand in cash, the rings and watches. I counted out three thousand to take with us on the trip and put the rest in the box. I had left the car at home and Uncle Fred was disappointed because we had to take the train. I explained to him that there was a war on and gasoline was rationed. I had used up all the gas coupons Bob had given me from his Merchant Marine ration and I hadn't applied for any. I think my allotment was five gallons a week. Hell, that wouldn't last me a night. I was driving a Buick, were they nuts?

We caught the three-forty train out of the Union Station and we were on our way to F.L.A., land of oranges, pretty girls, lots of sunshine and bugs. We had dinner in the dining car around six and then settled in for the night. Uncle Fred went to sleep right away but I was too excited. This was my first trip to Florida and I could see myself walking down a sandy beach, getting a tan, while my friends up north were freezing their buns off. I'd send them all cards with me on a sunny beach with two scantily covered girls in bathing suits. I didn't care what it cost me, but I was going to get those cards sent. After counting ten thousand railroad crossings with their dinging bells, I fell asleep. Believe it when I say this: Some guy in a white uniform came strolling through the car at six in the morning. The idiot was calling, "Breakfast, breakfast. Breakfast is now being served in the dining car." He needed a white jacket with strings attached.

For two days I endured crying kids, fat, flirting women and that nut in the white uniform. When we got off at Miami, I made up my mind that, if I ever went on another trip, I would take the Buick. Screw the gas coupons. I'd syphon the friggin' gas.

We checked into a small hotel in N.W. Miami, just a few miles from the beach. It was a nice room with a view, twin beds and a small stove and table in case you wanted to eat at home. I asked the clerk at the front desk when we arrived, "Where's the pool?"

"Three miles to the east, Sir. It's called the Atlantic Ocean."

"Gee, they float ships in your pool, huh?"

I guess he liked my sense of humor because we got friendlier. "I suggest, if you want to have a good time in Miami, Sir, you would find it more to your liking in a little place down the block called *The Eightball*. They have a bookie, they have a pool room and they have the ladies."

This guy spoke like an English gentleman and I figured he came from somewhere in the north-eastern part of the country.

"I bet they got a guy checking I.D., too." I didn't drink and it really didn't matter. Now take the ladies and the bookie, that was another story. But if you can't get in the joint for one, you can't get in for the others.

"Have you got a draft card, Sir? That would be all you need."

"I've just got a temporary driver's license from Illinois. It says I'm seventeen. I guess that's not too good, huh?"

"What part of Illinois, Sir?"

"Chicago."

"That's where I'm from, too." Suddenly, the Sir was gone and we laughed at that. He was from the north side, up around Belmont Avenue. He knew a few of the guys I went to the Parental School with and I felt right at home with him. I told him I was going to be eighteen the following day and asked if he wanted to go trick and treating with me.

"Let's go chick and treating," he suggested. "I know of two sisters, they're twins. Would you like to meet them?"

"Can we go to the beach?"

"We can go anyplace you want to, it's your birthday."

"What about this place where the bookie is, how old do you have to be to get in?"

"If you have a five dollar bill, that would be sufficient, Sir."

"Then I'm sufficient, Sir."

"The girls will go for that in a big way. They'll think you're a gangster from Chicago. That gets them every time." He thought for a moment. "I can rent a car from a buddie for a *saw-buck*,* can you handle that?"

"Yeah, I can get the dough from my Uncle Fred. He's paying for the trip, so he can pay for the ride."

"Okay, I'll see you tomorrow then. Meet you here at seven. I'll call the gals and get it all arranged. Ah, by the way, what's your name?"

"John, John Dekker. You remember that name. Remember everything and anything we do while I'm in Miami. It's important."

He shook my hand. "You got it, John Dekker. You take a leak, I'll remember it. I don't know what your game is, but it's all right with me. And, in case you want to know, my name's Slats. My first name's really Sidney, but I don't like that and all my friends call me Slats."

He was rail thin and it was understandable that he be called Slats. His face was ruddy complected with deep brown eyes and a sharp nose that came to a little ball at the end. He was only around twenty years old, but I felt he'd been around a little, just like me. It was like we went to different schools together. I liked the guy right off the bat and shook his hand as I left. In my hand was a twenty dollar bill.

He looked at me strangely and asked, "What's this for, John Dekker, you don't owe me nothing."

"That's so you can buy me a birthday present, Slats. See ya."

* *Saw-buck: Ten dollar bill.*

I had just reached the door when he called to me. "Yo, John! That's tomorrow night at seven. I'm a working man, you know."

I was glad he let me know that. I was figuring seven in the morning. "At night, what are we going to do on the beach at night?"

"I can see you're a south side boy, John Dekker. What we're going to do is play ships. You know how to play ships?"

"Ships . . . ?"

"Yeah, me and you are submarines. The girls are the ships. We try to sink them with our torpedoes."

"Yeah, well you can play around like that, Slats, but I'm going to try and screw one of them"

"You're kidding me . . .?"

"Sure, I'm kidding you. You think I'm serious? Hell, I know we don't got any torpedoes." I waved goodbye and walked out the door.

I ran with Slats every night for two weeks and we had a ball. He knew every swinging joint in Miami and we hit every one of them. Half the joints tried to card me, but when the doorman saw Slats, he passed us through, no questions. Most of the morning and afternoon hours, Uncle Fred and I spent in the pool room and bookie joint. He lost at the tables and I lost on the nags. At the end of two weeks I had gone through half of my money and decided to return to the Windy City. Slats halfway convinced me to stay over another week, but I had enough of Miami, so I declined. We made an agreement between us that we would get together in Chicago in the Springtime, when the tourist season fell off and there was more money to be made in snowbird country. On the day we left he saw us off at the train station.

"Don't forget, Slats. John Dekker. You know where I pissed and stuff. I may need you someday."

"Like in front of a jury?"

"Something like that."

"You got it, John. Only I'll feel a little embarrassed telling them about the night of the torpedoes."

As we got on the train, I thought of an answer for that and whispered into his ear, "Slats, there's more than one way to sink a ship."

We arrived back in Chicago two days later. I had only one complaint. That same nut in the white coat kept waking us up to eat. I don't think he ever slept. I know we didn't. When we hit Chicago, it was snowing. There was about five inches on the ground and it was coming down heavy. So there we were, Uncle Fred in short sleeves and a Panama hat, me in a light jacket. It turned out to be one of the worse snow storms in a decade. Great for burglars, but bad news for two sunburned tourists just in from Miami.

I learned something that day from my Uncle Fred that I would like to share with you people from Chicago. Uncle Fred, in his wisdom, said, "When the first snow storm hits Chicago, you measure how many inches fell. For every inch that fell, you can calculate how many snow storms will follow in that year," which means we were in for one hell of a winter.

It took us about twelve hours to get home from the loop. Any other time it would take an hour and a half, but the street cars inched their way through the snow and the snow plows were having a ball trying to keep the streets clear. It was gain an inch and lose a block all night long. By morning, according to the weather bureau, we had seventeen inches of snowfall throughout the night. You know, that would make a lot of snowmen.

We got home around two in the morning and I didn't get up until two the next afternoon. I thought it was that guy with the white coat that shook me awake, but is was my mother.

"Jonathan . . . " She was pissed.

"Yeah, Ma?"

"Don't you 'Yeah, Ma' me. I'm your mother!" Yep, she was pissed. "You think you can get away with anything. I suppose you think the flowers you wired me on your birthday changes things, well, it doesn't. You're still a spoiled brat and I'm ticked off."

I never would have guessed that. I had an idea where the flowers came from, dummy me. Why didn't I think of it? It had to be Uncle Fred that sent them. Come to think of it, he didn't get me a thing for my birthday, or did he . . . ?

I called up 718 three or four times during the day, but no Dugan or Bob. I called up the Normal Grill, no answer. The city was at a standstill. Nothing was moving. The Buick was completely covered with snow, it would be senseless to try driving it. All the neighborhood side streets were completely blocked off. You'd have to put snowshoes on the car to get through. The snow plows were out on the main streets working all day and into late evening. They were winning the battle, but losing the war, another front was coming in and promised another three inches during the night. It wasn't all bad, though. Think of all the overtime they would get.

It was the same thing the next day. Dad didn't go to work, so we cleaned the sidewalks and cleared the cars of snow. The skies cleared that night and the radio reported it was time to dig out. Dad and I had done all the digging we were going to do. Now it was up to the snow plows to get on the neighborhood streets. They came like a herd of elephants during the night and by morning the streets were fit to drive on. I got up early, saw the streets were clear and got out of the house as fast as I could. I was like a whore in church, I had to get out of there.

The Buick started with no trouble at all, it purred. While it warmed up, I cleared away the rest of the snow.

I knew dad had worked on it while I was in Miami. There was no way I could repay him because my dad wasn't that kind of guy. He did the tune-up because he wanted to. He did not expect payment for it. He probably enjoyed doing it.

One thing about a Chicago snow storm you can count on, nine months after the storm, almost half of the married couples in the area will be pregnant. What is there about a snow storm that does that? Well, I didn't have to worry about what the weather would do to me, I was back on the *Sun Times*, thanks to a rejuvenated Fredie. And I really mean that. Thanks Fredie!

I saw Helen at the grill four or five times in the two weeks I'd been back. She had her own apartment, which she shared with Fredie, also a steady job at the grill. The few times we talked eased my mind concerning her dad and the burglary. He did not report the burglary to the police for two reasons: one, he could not explain where all the money had come from, and two, if he did report it, Helen was going to inform the police about the heroin. Her father was between a rock and a hard place, no doubt about that. Her father could probably have beat the rap, but who wants heat like that? It was get even time for Helen, and she did a good job. What do they say? "What goes around, comes around."

Three weeks had passed and Dugan still had not called. He knew my phone number and I couldn't figure it out. Bob had returned to pick up his belongings at 718. He was in for a day and then he went back to Iowa to marry Kay Kay. He told me the eight thousand smackers he had from the score was going to be his down payment on a small farm and that was going to be his life style from now on. To each his own, and I was happy for him.

Dugan, he bought the farm, too. I finally received a letter from him via Sing Sing Prison, New York:

> Dear John,
> I would have written sooner or called you, but I've been in the slammer for the last month. I lost all the dough I had on the horses the first week we were here, so I decided to stick up a bookie. John, you won't believe it, there were twelve plain clothesmen in that joint. I think they were on my jury, too, because I got ten to fifteen years. If you see Bob, please tell him about the bum rap I got. Damn, the gun wasn't even real, John, and they hit me with a jolt like that, there ain't no justice. Anyway, send my best to Bob and Kay Kay. Vi's on a bus heading for Chicago now, she

*stuck with me till the last day. She said she'd wait for me and she's crazy enough to do it. Talk her out of that shit, John, okay?*

*Well, I'll see you down the line, not this line though, till then, I'd appreciate it if you'd write me once in a while and maybe send me enough for cigs and the Chicago paper, I want to keep up with the ponies while I'm here. When I get home, I'm going to have one hell of a system.*

*Your pal, Dugan.*

That made my month of November. No Helen, Bob was going to save the nation with Iowa corn-fed beef, and Dugan, poor Dugan, had retired for the duration of the war and then some.

I called Bob the day after I got Dugan's letter. He didn't take the news too well. We agreed to send Dugan a little money every month while he was locked up. We figured twenty dollars a month ought to take care of anything he might need, coffee, cigarettes and the daily paper. Bob suggested that Vi should come and visit with them in Iowa until she got her life straightened out. I thought it was a good idea and promised to mention it to her when she got to Chicago.

I thought it was a great idea. Chances are she'd meet a nice guy and settle down. I was sure going to mention it.

*Chapter 11*

## "My Space"

Events came to a crawl as Christmas approached. This was the time of the year when most thieves were in full swing, Christmas presents had to be bought or stolen and thieves preferred the latter. It's a known fact, more banks are robbed during the holidays than at any other time. Burglary turns epidemic and doubles. Car theft goes down, nobody wants a hot car for Christmas. All in all, Christmas is a very active season for thieves. Me, I broke all the rules. I went out and bought my Christmas presents. I hope nobody finds out about that.

I was still living with my mother and father but planned to move in with Uncle Fred after we brought in the New Year. Things at home were all right, but I was not working. I had nice clothes and I drove a gas eater. My mother never did come right out with it, but I felt she suspected I was getting my spending money from the tooth fairy. She or my dad could not accuse me of stealing, because I was always home in the daytime. When I went out at night, it was usually with Billy or my sis, Toots. We'd take in a movie and then have burgers and fries as an encore. We were always home early, so Ma and Dad were left playing a guessing game. There are not many kids eighteen years of age that had a bankroll like I had. In those days you worked for a buck and a half an hour. I had six thousand in cash, plus the bag of rings and box of pocket watches in my poke.

You won't believe this, but I was having trouble spending it. I had to play it poor, no flashing of money. I had learned that lesson the hard way. There should be a message in here for all would-be thieves. Either learn now to invest your money or get into a business as a front. You'd be surprised how many thieves went into a legitimate business and made a success out of it.

Politicians seem to work this formula in reverse, but they have things mixed up half of the time anyway. Take a lawyer, he works his butt off defending a client, he researches the law book, seeks out witnesses, checks evidence and then brings his client to trial. Well done, counselor. You earned your fee, but you lost your case. Your only mistake was you did not arrange to see the judge first. Had you talked to him, you probably could have paid him off and got your case dismissed. But you learn through the years and one day you are a judge. On that day, do you decide to take the bribes offered you, or do you remain the businessman? We all know this is fiction, right? Wrong.

All in all, I've been on the wrong side of the law for twenty-eight years and I've paid off a few cops, a few judges, and a barrel of lawyers. I even tried the F.B.I. once, but that was a waste of time, but I'll bet it's been done or will be someday. I think the funniest bribe I was in on . . . Oh, oh, I'm getting ahead of my story. I'll tell you about that later.

I moved in with Uncle Fred two weeks before Christmas. This didn't set right with my mother, but I had to have space. I was growing up and I wanted to be on my own. Dad agreed with me and convinced Ma it was all right. After all, I would be just a mile or so away with Uncle Fred. What was the harm in it? She agreed on one condition. I would have dinner with them every Sunday and no excuses. Hell, I planned it that way anyway. There was one thing I liked about living with Uncle Fred, I could come and go as I pleased, no questions asked.

His apartment fit the situation perfectly. It was located within three blocks of the Normal Grill and two blocks from the pool room, my favorite haunts. We had two bedrooms, a bath and a large kitchen, just enough room to keep out of each other's way. Uncle Fred was more or less a loner, anyway, and above all, he tended to mind his own business. He knew I had money. He also knew I was not working, but he never questioned me. I made a deal with him when I moved in; I would pay the rent, one hundred dollars a month, *chump change,** I would also pay for the groceries. He, in turn, would keep the apartment clean and do the laundry. Uncle Fred would always go to the pool room around six at night and return about eleven. He would then read his paper, drink a cup of coffee, eat a donut and retire for the night. On one particular evening, I noticed something about him, he was holding the paper at arms length and squinting his eyes.

"Hey, Uncle Fred!"

"Yes," he turned to me, still squinting. "You said something, Johnny?"

"Don't you wear glasses when you read? If you held that paper any further away, it would be in the next room."

I let it go at that and made up my mind we would see an eye doctor the next day. No wonder Uncle Fred was losing at pool. He hadn't lost his stroke, he was blind as a bat without glasses. It took three days to get him his glasses, he needed bifocals, and from that day on, he couldn't be touched at the tables. All them old sharks had met one bad tad-pole after Uncle Fred got his cheaters.

* *Chump change: Small amount of money.*

*Chapter 12*

# "I Just Did It"

Don't ask me why I did it, I just did it. Maybe it was boredom, maybe it was the scent of excitement, maybe it was just
crazy. I guess I was just bored-crazy. It could have been from
too many pool halls and too many hamburgers. You get in a
rut like that and anything can happen. Ray Panozzo, brother
of Victor Panozzo, son of Tony Panozzo, employee of the
D.M.V., and I met at the Rosebowl Bowling Alley one night
just as the place was closing. Ray and I had gone to school together and he knew just about what kind of guy I was. Fact
was, every student in school knew it. One thing about my
chosen profession, your reputation follows you. I noticed Ray
as he walked up the steps to the lobby of the bowling alley. A
bowling ball in one hand, his bowling shoes in the other.

"Hey, Po-nose-so," I called to him.

He stopped dead in his tracks, but did not turn around.
He began to sing a tune, "Sailing, sailing over Niagara Falls.
Captain Dekker, lost his pecker, looking for his balls." He
then dropped his bowling ball and shoes on the steps, turned
around and smiled.

"Johnny Dekker, when did you get out of jail? My dad told
me you was around getting fixed up with a lot of stuff at the
D.M.V. How come you didn't come to see me when you got
home?" He tried to look hurt.

"I thought I was your paizon?"

Ray looked the same, long red hair combed slick on both
sides with a curl hanging to the center of his forehead. His
eyes were brownish red, just like his hair, his nose came to a
sharp point. He was one of the few people I've met, that could

touch his nose with his tongue. How many of you readers are trying to do that right now?

"Red Head, I meant to stop in to see you many times, but I've been tied up lately. Business, stuff like that." I couldn't tell him I'd been on a crime wave.

"Business?"

I picked up his bowling ball bag and shoes and started up the stairs. He walked beside me until we reached the front door. We stopped and faced each other. "Business?" he repeated.

When we got outside there was a stiff wind and it was cold. I pointed to the Buick at the curb. "Monkey business, Ray. You wouldn't be interested. You got a ride home? That's my heap at the curb."

"Yes, I would. I'd be interested and I would like a lift home."

We got in the car, started it and headed south to where he lived. I knew where the house was and drove right to it. I knew Ray was boiling over to ask me what I was talking about. He really wasn't nosy, it was just that I made it sound so mysterious. People tend to get like that when you leave them hanging without an answer to their question.

"Ray, I can't tell you what I've been doing. Nobody knows what I've been doing. Now, if I told you what I was doing and someday it got out to the cops, then I'd wonder if you told them. So, if I don't tell you, then, if I get picked up by the cops, I'll know it wasn't you that told them, because I didn't tell you. You understand?"

"You're as crazy as ever, John. Let me out of here." He got out of the car. He was mumbling to himself, he started to close the door but stopped. "John, call me tomorrow, you got my number. I got something you might be interested in. Now go home and cut out some dolls, you nut."

"You're on Red Head, I'll call you around two."

"And John, no more of that double talk. You're gunna have me cutting out dolls."

I called, as promised, at two the next afternoon. Ray's mother answered the phone and we chatted for about twenty minutes before Ray saved me. Lina Panozzo was quite a talker, she didn't speak very good English, but what she had in her vocabulary she used to the fullest. She was also the very best cook on the south side of Chicago. Uncle Fred was the worst cook on the south side, and when she invited me to dinner that night, I could not refuse.

"You bet, Mrs. Panozzo. I'll be there at six sharp. And, thank you."

Ray wanted me to come over right away, but I begged off with the excuse that I wanted to catch the last races as Sportsman Park. I told him I had a hot one in the ninth race and I didn't want to miss it. The truth was, I had planned to take a ride over to the Rumbell Real Estate and take an inventory of my goodies. They had been in the safe deposit box over two months now and I had no idea what I had in the leather bag with the rings. I got there at three-thirty on the dot and was met by an elderly man in his sixties. He was dressed in a business suit, gray in color, as was his hair. He was standing at the door as I entered. On his right was a woman of about the same age typing a memo or something. There was nobody else in the building. I glanced around casually, "About ready to close?" I asked.

"Half hour to go, son, and that's it for the day." he answered.

I pointed to the vault, "I'm just going to be here a minute or two, Sir. I want to get some coins out of my box."

"Coin collector, huh?"

"Yes, Sir. I've got some real nice Indian pennies. I've been saving since I was six years old. Got some V nickels, too."

"That's good, son. You keep saving those coins, someday they will be worth a lot."

"Yes, Sir."

I followed him to the vault and we went in. The woman at the desk didn't pay any attention to us, she just kept typing and humming to herself. I handed him my key, he glanced at it and took a key from off a hook in the vault. He inserted both keys in my box and swung it open, he then went to the desk where the woman was typing. I took the bag of rings out of the box and slipped them into a small paper bag. I called to him. "Okay, Sir. I'm done here, you can close it up."

He walked back to the vault quickly and I thought he was pretty quick for a man of his age. He closed the door on my box and returned the key to me. He then walked me back to the front door, patted me on the shoulder, and wished me a good day.

My mind was spinning as I drove back to the apartment. What a set up! There had to be two hundred safe deposit boxes in that vault and the only thing that stood between them and a good crew, was two old people. I decided, without a moment's hesitation, this place had to go down. I would watch it for a few weeks and then sell it to the best bidder at 10%. No way was I going to do it myself. Real pro's had to take down this caper. I could only see one problem. I didn't know any pro's. The only person I knew with any class was the Sheik. I decided to talk to him, just feel him out. What did I have to lose? Besides, my gut feeling told me Sheik knew a hell of a lot more than he put on. I hate guys like that.

Ray met me at the front door and I could smell Mrs. Panozzo's spaghetti clear across the house. I sniffed a few times in the air, rubbed my hands together and said, "Mama, Mia, only your mother can make spaghetti like that."

Ray cut me short. "My sister made it."

"Only your sister can make spaghetti like that," I countered.

"I'm putting you on, John. Ma don't like you and she went to the movies. I made the spaghetti. Ma thinks you're a hoodlum, my sister, Carol, hates you because you treat her like a little girl. And I think we ought to go to the White Castle for some sliders and forget this whole messed up night."

If you've never been in one of Chicago's White Castles, then you don't know what a slider is. They are delicious, they are greasy, they are the size of two silver dollars. Two bites and they are gone, they slide down your throat and land in your belly with a thud. You order ten at a time. They're only 5 cents each and they sell them by the millions. We ordered twenty sliders and two coffees to go. On a good night, it is the wise man who chooses to eat his sliders out in the parking lot. I am a wise man, besides, I wanted to talk to Ray in private, and a White Castle on a good night was anything but private.

We slid our hamburgers down in about ten minutes. You have to chew them, you see. If you didn't, you would be in trouble for a week. The oil fields in Texas do not produce as much gas in a week, as a slider does in an hour. It's an art, believe me.

I lit a cigarette, belched and looked at Ray. I did not beat around the bush with him, I got right to the point. "What's your deal Redhead, what have you got that might interest me?"

"A truckload of tires," he explained. "Every Saturday night I've been taking one or two tires from this truck they park behind the bowling alley. I sell them to Tony Peanuts for five bucks each. With the war on, it's hard to get tires. I figure you and me can knock down the whole truck and clean up. What'a ya think of that, John, is that great or what?"

"Ray, let me ask you one question."

"Shoot."

"When did you decide to become a thief?"

"What'a ya mean, John?"

"Let me put it this way. You're not cut out for this life. You're a good student, you have no record with the cops and, with Vic in the Marine Corps., you're all your mother's got. You go to jail and she's got nothing. So I'm turning down your deal and no hard feelings."

Ray was not hurt, he looked defeated, like a dream that didn't turn out right. There was no doubt he had been counting on me to come in with him on this score and I let him down, but I felt there was something else behind it, too. So I popped the question, "You're not telling me everything, Ray. You got a problem?"

"Damn, John. I got problems on top of problems. I need money. I got this girl pregnant and I can't get it fixed on two tires at a time. I need three hundred bucks and I need it fast."

I started the car, punched it into gear and headed for my apartment. Ten minutes later, I handed Ray the money he needed.

"Here, Ray, you owe me sixty tires. Stay away from that truck. I'll let you know when I need them."

The next two weeks proved very interesting. Besides checking out the safe deposit box caper, I found out Sheik, indeed, had connections. It had been easy and he went for my story hook, line and sinker. My story wasn't hard to believe, it happens every day in one way or another. People lose their rings and people find them, simple as that. Could I help it if I found one in a vault while looking over my coins. Sheik didn't think so, either, and thought I was very lucky. It was a handsome ring, perhaps a quarter carat, blue/white and brilliant. I had checked at a local jewelry store as to what it was worth retail and found if I wanted to replace it, it would run in the neighborhood of two hundred and fifty dollars.

Sheik offered me a *C-note* * and I thought that was more than fair. Stan, the fence, would have offered me twenty-five bucks and cried for a month. Any honest fence pays about 25% on the dollar.

Sheik paid me the hundred and I managed to stay away from the grill for three days before I laid down the clincher on him. This time I showed up with the box of pocket watches. I left them on the floor board of the car while I went in to speak to him. Ten minutes later we were riding down 119th Street and he was looking over the watches.

"Find these in the vault, too, John?" he asked, tracing his finger over a design on one of the watches.

I hit him cold. "I stole them just before I went to Florida. They're for sale. You interested?"

He counted the watches, there were sixteen. "I'll give you eight hundred. They're probably worth more, but I don't

* *C-note: One Hundred dollar bill.*

know anything about watches. Anyway, that's my deal. What do you say?"

"Done."

"I'll give you the money tomorrow, John. I haven't got that much cash on me right now. You can hold the watches until I pay you or you can let me have them now. It's up to you."

"You take the watches and I'll see you next week for the money. I'll be gone for about a week, so you do what you gotta do."

We pulled up to the curb. He put eight watches in each of his overcoat pockets and left the box on the floorboard. He waved to me as he entered the grill. I was about to pull away when Helen and Fredie walked out of the Grill. Fredie was helping Helen with her coat and I noticed she was putting on weight and it wasn't from eating. Oh, no, Helen was going to be a mommy. Damn, I envied that Fredie, he was a real machine.

The week went fast, Uncle Fred and I played nine million games of eight ball and I beat him once. How can you play one solid week of pool and win only one game? And do you want to know something? I'll bet Uncle Fred took a dive in the game I won, because I lost the next thirty-six in a row. Me thinks Uncle Fred hustled his favorite nephew.

I called Sheik and he told me to stop by the grill after closing. I could tell from the tone of his voice that we were going to make a deal of some sort, or perhaps, he just didn't want to pay me off during business hours. I waited outside in the car until the lights of the grill went out and then I went to the front door. It was locked, I tapped on the glass with my car key and Sheik opened up for me. There was only a night light on and the place seemed like a tomb without the juke box blaring. Sheik pointed to the back booth where coffee was set up. There was also a large plate of steaming fries. He took the seat across from me and tossed me a money clip with eight one hundred dollar bills in it. I slipped the money out of the clip and handed it back to him. He waived his hand in protest.

"The clip is yours, John. You gave me a very good deal and I appreciate it. The watches are first class and are quite an addition to my collection. If you come across any more, see me first, okay sport?"

I almost choked on a french fry. "You kept them?" I couldn't believe it. "You didn't sell them . . . You got a collection?"

So much for gut feelings. "Sheik, I've got a lot of stuff I want to unload. But I have to talk to people in the business that can handle things like that."

"Things like what?"

"Like a leather bag full of rings, like the one I sold you. To be honest with you, Sheik, I was thinking you might know someone in the rackets that would be interested in a big score. But I guess I'm wrong, huh?"

"Wrong as rain, John. I don't know anybody except me. I bought the watches and I knew they were hot, that makes me crooked, I guess. But I'm the only person that knows we made this deal, except you, and I want it to stay that way. Any time more than two people know something, then you can bet someone else will find out. That's a good rule to follow, John."

"I'll give that a lot of thought, Sheik. In the meantime, do you want to look over the bag of rings?"

"What kind of money are we talking, John?"

"I've got over sixty rings, diamonds in all of them. I want four thousand for the lot of them. We're talking over ten grand wholesale. It's a hell of a deal for someone that knows where to get rid of them. That's my trouble. Right now, I don't know that somebody, you don't know that somebody and that somebody don't know us. Anyway, it's a good deal, if you want it, Sheik, it's yours."

"I haven't got that kind of money, John."

That answered my question. I was disappointed. My safe deposit box caper was still up in the air and I had a bag of diamond rings that were looking for a home. This is what you call experience. What I learned from this was, never go for anything except money. Anything that hasn't got a picture of a

president on it, forget it. Money, you don't have to sell to anyone. Rings, bonds, cars and even your body, you have to sell.
Money, you just spend. Go into a grocery store sometime and
order five pounds of pork chops, now try to pay for them with
a ring. The guy will think you're nuts. Now offer him a ten
dollar bill, he'll throw his jaw out of joint with a smile.

I saw Ray Panozzo the next night. He thanked me again
for helping him out with his parenthood problem. I asked
him how the tire business was going. I was happy to hear he
had retired, then I showed him the bag of rings. His eyes grew
larger as he poured them onto the table. In the over-hanging
light, they glowed white fire with every color of the rainbow
escaping. I didn't say anything, I just watched as he picked one
of the rings from the pile. He held it to the light, turning it in
his fingers.

"Where . . . ?

"Never mind where, Ray," I said cutting him off. "The
thing is I got them and they're for sale. You see Tony Peanuts,
he'll like this better than tires. I want three grand, anything
over that is yours."

He placed the rings back into the bag, threw out his hand
and said, "You got a deal, John. Give me a few days. Tony will
love this. You'll have your three grand before the week's out."

"Ray," he was so happy, but I had to tell him.

"Yeah?"

"This is all I got. There ain't no more, so don't promise
Tony any more. And don't tell him where you got the stuff.
You might hurt his feelings, but he'll appreciate you keeping
your mouth shut about me."

"He won't even ask me, John. He didn't ask me about the
tires, so why should he ask about this?"

"These ain't tires, Ray. Just don't tell him, okay?"

"Okay, you got it. If he insists, I'll tell him I got them from
a guy that made a score on the north side. But he won't ask
me, I know Tony, and he don't ask questions."

Everything was going well. Ray paid me off and I had a ten
thousand dollar bankroll hidden in my father's basement. Less

than eighteen months since being released from the Chicago Parental School and I had more money than my dad made in a year. The difference was, my dad could spend his money and didn't have to explain to anyone where he got it. I, on the other hand, just couldn't throw money around. I would have liked to, but people get suspicious when you have no income. This leads to questions you cannot answer and often to the attention of our public servants. Don't get me wrong, a person cannot be incarcerated for having money. Fact is, you can tell the fuzz it's money you received from a crime, or you can tell them you got it from your grandma. Either way, they can't lock you up for it unless they can implicate you in a crime. No crime, no lockie up.

Like I said, I don't know why I did it. I just did it. I can only reason it was because I was bored stiff. My only friends were either in jail, or worse still, married. Bob had married Kay Kay during the Christmas holiday and Dugan began his second year in up-state New York, some place called Attica.

*Chapter 13*

---

## "Let There Be Honor"

---

You should have seen me all dressed up in my pretty navy blues with white booties. No, better yet, you should not have seen me, I was the sorriest looking sailor in the navy. But then, if you looked around me, I guess all the guys in boot camp looked the same. We were all confused, young and not used to taking orders from some old man with a bunch of medals on his chest.

Every morning, 5 a.m., "Up and at 'em, men. Time for your break-fast and a ten mile march."

That was ten miles each way. You were dead on your feet, hungry and ready to kill for lunch. No lunch, though, sorry, you missed lunch, sandwiches would have to do. And then, me hearties, we will fight fires the rest of the afternoon. I'll tell you one thing, this guy deserved all the medals he got. He drove us for six weeks: March, march, march. Blow the hell out of targets, fight fires and then march some more. Our C.P.O. was never happy. According to him, we were "the worst marchers in the entire navy." Two days before we were to graduate from the Great Lakes Naval Training Center, Chief Kiel informed us that we would be the head company on the parade grounds on graduation day. An honor given to the best marching company at the training center. I told you that Kiel was a son-of-a-gun. . . .

We each received a seven-day leave after boot camp and I felt like the cock-of-the-walk strutting down the street in my navy blues. For once in my life I had done something without screwing it up; I had completed what was very close to a six-week jail sentence without trying to break out. I probably would have broken out, but they trusted you and that took all the fun out of it. The other reason I didn't take it on the lam was because I was just to damn tired. You just don't "get up and go" after a twenty-mile march. I wonder if they planned it that way. I thought very seriously of not returning after my liberty was up, I also thought of cutting my throat, but common sense told me I'd be dead in any case.

While I was home I gave my dad the Buick and told him to do what he wanted with it. I explained to him that if I got out of this war alive, I would buy a new car because I planned to save every cent I could while I was in the navy. I knew, at the time I told him this, just how much money I would save while in the navy, ten thousand bucks, because that's how much I had in my stash. I told him I expected to do a lot of gambling while I was away. Each month I would send him my winnings home and he could put it in the bank for me. Winning was no problem, I explained, I'll cheat.

I returned to base and within three days I was on my way to Camp Elliot, California, a tent city, just outside of San Diego. Navy life changed quickly, there were no more marches, just sleep, eat and go on liberty until we were shipped out. You talk about dull: San Diego was the worse liberty town in the United States. It seemed every sailor in the fleet was stationed in San Diego, there were ten swabbies for every girl in town and I had a hard time staying out of trouble. I always had a gal on each arm and a bundle of cash in my pocket. I drove a rented car and I spent my money freely. The guys in my outfit thought I was a show-off, but none of them refused to go on a double date with me, even if I told them it was a blind date. Two things about money, one, you make a lot of friends, two, girls seem to like you better if you got MONEY!

Liberty was great in San Diego, great if you liked carnivals, movies and the zoo. I appreciated all three, but not every night. Unfortunately, I and two of my buddies decided to go to San Pedro on a San Diego pass and got caught by the S.P.s on the way back to San Diego. We were six hours over our liberty pass and we each received a *Captain's Mast*.* Our sentence

* *Captain's Mast: Minor court martial*

was twenty-four hours of extra duty and no liberty for thirty days. The twenty-four hours of extra duty consisted of one hour of work each night for twenty-four nights: sweeping floors, washing trucks, spearing cigarette butts from the camp grounds and washing pots and pans. The first night I washed a truck. The second night I went A.W.O.L.

I reached Chicago five days later. I called my dad and it came as no surprise to find the S.P.s had paid a visit to my house the third day I was over the hill. For the next three weeks I stayed at Uncle Fred's, always looking over my shoulder, just waiting for them to pounce on me. As I reflect upon it, I must have kicked my butt a thousand times for this stupid act, but it was too late. The way I figured it, I'd just hang around until they nailed me and take whatever punishment I had coming to me.

It didn't take long. A week later the war was over and I, like a hundred million other people, went out and got blasted out of our skulls. On V.J. night I landed in the brig at Great Lakes. It seemed like every sailor in the navy ended up in the brig that night. All I remember is, I woke up with the grand-daddy of all hang-overs and three of the ugliest marine guards looking down at me. They were smiling. Each had a billy-club with a rawhide loop at the end of it and these three jarheads gave one scared sailor a demonstration in how to twirl a billy-club. I kept my mouth shut. These guys meant bad trouble on my head if I even looked like I was a wise guy. Marine guards run the navy brigs. They are bred to hate sailors, and, if you are a marine in the brig, you are in real trouble. I've got to be honest. I was never beat up by a marine guard; I was pushed, kicked and tossed around, but never actually hurt. On the other hand, I witnessed many beatings to marine prisoners by their marine keepers.

It's hard to believe, but the day I came up for my Summary Court Martial, I was the happiest guy in the world. One way or another I was going to get out of the brig. Either I was going to a naval prison or I was going back to active duty. The hearing only lasted fifteen minutes. I pleaded guilty to being over the hill twenty-six days, (four days short of desertion) and was given the option of either a bad conduct discharge or returning to duty. With the bad conduct discharge I would be released that day and allowed to go home. Returning to duty would mean I would still be stuck with the navy. It could be months, it could be years. The trial took fifteen minutes, my decision took fifteen seconds.

I was discharged from the United States Navy on July 14th, 1947. On my chest was a gold ruptured duck and in my hand was an Honorable Discharge. I've never regretted my decision. . .

*Chapter 14*

## "From Time To Time"

The summer of 1947 went swiftly. With the money I sent my dad every month, I managed to buy a 1947 Buick convertible. I was the envy of every young girl and guy in the neighborhood. Everybody wanted to be the friend of Johnny Dekker; I always had money in my pocket and I must have been one whale of a poker player, because I won enough in the navy to buy the car. That's what I wanted them to think and it worked beautifully. There was only one question asked now, "How did you do in the poker game Saturday night, John?" What poker game? I made my money the hard way, I stole it.

I was working with a fella by the name of Dominick. He was short, around five foot five and muscular, a real hard gent, if provoked, otherwise, a real softy. We had been hitting loan companies throughout Chicago, maybe one a week for about two months. One day we got stopped on the street because we resembled two other men in the same business. It amazed me to know there were two other men in this world as ugly as Dominick and me. We explained to the police that we were not the fellas they wanted, and I think we had them convinced until they found the .32 automatic in my jacket pocket. We were not convicted of any robberies, because nobody fingered us in the show-ups, but the judge decided I be found guilty for impersonating a police officer and I was given a ten-month sentence in the Chicago House of Detention. This establishment was also known as the Bridewell, a bug-ridden, smelly, rundown piece of vomit they called a jail. Its clientele consisted of mostly drunks, purse snatchers, jackrollers and the scum off the streets of Chicago. Dominick was lucky. He got a year in the County Jail, that means he did a lucky. He got a year in the County Jail, that means he did a month more time than me, but he did it with a class prisoner. I was released in August 1948.

Two weeks later I met Bunny while cruising down the street. I was with my new partner, Bob "Mike" Roman. Mike was the kind of a guy everybody liked, he was a soft, smooth talker, not handsome, by any means, but beautiful inside and with a personality that could charm the devil himself. Mike had guts, but no sense; he wasn't really wild, just high strung when it came to a bank robbery. Although he never hurt anyone, I always feared that the day would come when he lost his cool. So far, it had not arrived, but with Mike, you never knew.

Rosemary "Bunny" Hinkle was designed in a fashion that would fulfill any man's fantasy. I first spotted her walking down the street with another girl. It was a warm summer night, bright with stars and a full moon. We were cruising in the Buick, roof down and Mike sending out wolf calls to anything wearing skirts. He spotted Bunny and the other girl and let out a howl that could be heard half way across town. Neither Bunny or the other girl turned around. Mike gave them his best, but they paid no attention and walked into an ice cream parlor. I found the first parking spot I could and pulled in.

They were sitting in a booth next to the juke box. I tried to act like they weren't even there. Mike wanted to sit down with them, but I pointed to the booth across from them and said, "Down boy, you're drooling at the mouth."

Can you believe it, these two broads didn't look at us once. I thought for a moment they were mutes. "Forget them," I said to myself, "What wasn't to be, wasn't to be." I drank my hot chocolate and decided it was time for Mike and I to leave. As we were walking past their booth, Mike leaned over and picked up their bill.

"My treat, girls. See you tomorrow, same time, okay?"

Without waiting for an answer, he walked straight to the cash register, paid the bills and we walked out. I tried to exanything to do with us, they didn't even know we were alive, we had struck out, nothing, zipp, zero.

We got into the car and he turned to me. "Eight to five says they'll be there tomorrow night, John. Is it a bet?"

"Bet."

As we were driving past the ice cream parlor the two girls came walking out. We caught the red light and I forced my eyes to look straight ahead. No way in the world would I turn my head, not for a million dollars. This guy had his pride and he meant to keep it.

"Are you going toward 95th Street?" Bunny asked. "If you are, I would sure appreciate a ride."

So much for the pride and million dollars. "Sure, hop in," I answered. "That's right on my way."

Mike opened the door for them and they got into the back seat. He smiled at me and held out his hand. "That will be a five spot, John. Thank you."

We took them home. It was a three-story apartment building on 95th Street and Cottage Grove Avenue. A rundown neighborhood and completely out of contrast with the way Bunny and Barbara were dressed. Had I not known, I would have sworn these two girls lived on the gold coast of Chicago and not living in what would become slums in the near future. Bunny was dressed in a light, short sleeve summer dress, bright red in color with a galaxy of dark black polka dots. It fit her like a band aid and displayed a perfectly developed body. Her hair was strawberry blonde with ringlets and her eyes were bluish green. She wore very little makeup, a touch of mascara, a dab of lipstick. She needed no makeup, to me she was five foot nine inches of what I'd been waiting for all my life.

There was very little cruising after that. Bunny and I became man and wife on November 27th, 1948. Our twin girls, Dawn and Donna, four pounds, three ounces each, were brought into the world on April 27th, 1949. It was a medical miracle, and of course, we told everyone that didn't believe us that we had been married secretly in 1947. I am sorry to say, they all thought we were full of bull hockey.

Our little girls were really the ones who suffered through this union of misfit parents. Bunny tried hard to make a success out of our marriage and her only mistake was going along with my high-flying ways of living, and for this, our little girls paid dearly. Had I been a man, I would have broken off my relationship with Mike, settled down and went to work, but no, I was the kind of person that believed that manual labor was for the suckers in this world or some Mexican hillbilly. In the second year of our marriage, it was over. I was standing trial for nine bank robberies. I don't bum-rap anybody, but if Mike would have kept his mouth shut, there might have been a chance we would have beat the raps and I wouldn't have ended up in Leavenworth Penitentiary. I'll never forget what the Fed's told me.

"John, in the old days, it was a common practice for the authorities to beat a man to make him talk. In Mike Roman's case, we would have had to beat him up to keep him quiet."

Mike received ten years and almost threw-up in the courtroom. The judge asked him if he had anything to say after sentencing.

Mike replied, "I can't do all that time, your honor."

The judge had a sad smile on his face and responded, "You do what you can, son."

I got ten years, too, but ignored that gray-haired Judge, when he asked me if I had anything to say. I don't think he liked that.

*Chapter 15*

## "Good-Bye"

It usually took two weeks before a prisoner was shipped from the Cook County Jail to the U.S. Penitentiary, Leavenworth, Kansas. In the meantime, it was sit, wait and think. Thinking: that is the hard part of doing time. You can't take your mind off the outside. You can play cards, hold bull-sessions and even sleep, but, in some tiny part of your mind, you are thinking. Some men put on acts; they laugh and play all day long, pretending they don't care, so they got time, so what. Real tough people, but when mail call comes along or they don't get a visit, well, these same tough guys seem to melt a little. They don't laugh or play as hard and sometimes you don't see them for days.

I received mail from Bunny almost everyday, and on visiting day, she was never late. She was there promptly at nine a.m. and waiting in line. Our visits were short, we had to get everything said in a half hour. The visits were held in one large room separated by a steel wall with little cubby-hole windows. You could not talk in a normal voice, you had to yell at the top of your lungs to be heard on the other side of the window. Visits were demoralizing, they took away any dignity you had and completely humiliated your visitor. Your loved ones are always searched for contraband, made to wait, sometimes for hours, on a hard wooden bench and then allowed a half hour visit in a room completely enclosed in steel and windows an inch thick.

I don't blame our custodians for leaning on us a little heavy at times. I suppose we had it coming, but to put our visitors through such nickel and dime harrassment was a mockery to the criminal justice system. To put it plainly, it stunk!

After our first visit, I wrote Bunny a long letter. I told her to see my dad and get the title to the car. She could do what she wanted with it, sell it or keep it, it was her choice. We had about six thousand in the bank and I suggested she use that wisely until she got a job. It was a very difficult letter because for the first time in my life I was thinking of someone else and not myself. I asked her to forget me and get on with her life. I told her I would refuse any visits from now on and would send her mail back to her. I told her this is what I wanted. I had no choice in the matter and neither did she. She had the twins to worry about and I would just be a worthless hunk of garbage holding her back from a decent life. It was hard for me writing that letter, the big, bad, bank robber was crying. The next day I wrote a letter to the Warden of the Cook County Jail. It was short and sweet:

> Dear Warden,
> Please get me on a shipment to Leavenworth. If
> you don't, I'm going to kill somebody."

Two days later, I was on my way to Leavenworth.

*Chapter 16*

---

# "On The Road Again"

It's a two-day trip from Chicago to Leavenworth, Kansas, approximately five hundred miles. We probably could have made the journey in one day, but the weather was bad and the roads were as slick as a hound dog's tongue. The U.S. Marshall driving the car was in his late sixties. He drove the car with both hands on the wheel and slowed down at every curve. I had no complaint about that. I was in no hurry to reach our destination. This was to be the last time I would see the free world for a long time, and, if he wanted to go by the way of the Virgin Islands, it would be okay with me.

We stopped for the night in Springfield, Illinois, and were locked up in the holding tank at the county jail. One thing I can say about their jail in Springfield, they treat you decent. We were fed a meal of fried chicken, sour dough biscuits and country gravy. This was a real treat compared to the menu they served in the Cook County Jail. The county jail in Chicago usually served beans or stew; beans one day, stew the next, on the third day they mixed them together and it was called, soup.

We left early the next morning after donuts and coffee. The roads were much better for driving and we arrived in Leavenworth about three in the afternoon. The sun was in the west and the marshall, riding shotgun, pointed out the dome of Leavenworth. It was the color of gold in the glare of the sun.

"That's the Big Top, boys, over there on your right." He said it like he was trying to sell us some real estate.

I was not going to buy. You couldn't give me that joint. It made me sick to my stomach, just looking at it. We drove down a tree-lined road leading up to the big gray building. Leavenworth sits on a slight hill. On each side of the road are the warden's home and the senior officers' quarters. At the foot of Leavenworth are steps leading up to the main door. I didn't bother counting them as we went up. The marshalls handed over their weapons before we were allowed to enter the building and then the large doors yawned open. We were ushered through three more doors before our shackles were removed and we were then allowed to smoke. I glanced around and saw a prisoner mopping the floor. He studied us, smiled and said, "We got some new fish."

I smiled back at him, "Yeah, turkey, two tiger sharks."

"I was just kidding you, son. All new fellas are called fish when they first get here," he explained. "No harm meant."

He was an old guy, gray, about sixty. I realized I shouldn't have come down on him like that. He was probably happy to see a couple of new men and had just run off at his mouth.

"Sorry, dad," I apologized, "I just don't think I'm going to like my new quarters and I'm a little on edge right now." I stuck out my hand and he took it in his. "My name's John Dekker, and I'm sorry if I hurt your feelings."

"No harm done, kid. I know the feeling. I've been here a spell myself. My name's George Kelly. You have any problems with anybody, you just tell them you know me, and you'll be all right."

Our next stop was the clothing room. Here we were searched, showered, and fitted into our prison garb. We were then escorted to the fish bowl. This is a name given to the building that housed all new men. It could have been a navy barracks the way it was laid out. There were rows upon rows of bunks, with a foot locker at the end of each bed. In the center of the room was a large room complete with toilets, showers and mirrors. We were turned over to the officer on duty and he gave us a short rundown on what we could do, and what we could not do. There were great deal of no-do's and very little do's.

The next morning we were awakened to the sound of a bugle call, just like in the navy. We washed, dressed and were led off to breakfast. On the way to the mess hall, I spotted the old man that had been mopping the front hallway. He had been watching the line I was walking in and waved his hand at me as we passed.

"How ya doing, Johnny. Feel better today?"

"Okay, George." I felt like shit, "I'll see you when I get out of the fish tank."

"Yeah, hang in there, fish," he laughed, "I'll send you some cigarettes this afternoon." He walked away slowly and I knew I had found a friend.

The man walking next to me turned and looked at me strangely. It bothered me. "You got a problem, buddie?" I asked sharply.

"No, no, no problem," he said shyly. "Sorry for staring. I was just trying to figure out how a new guy like you would be knowing a fella like Machine Gun Kelly."

"It's easy to figure out," I said, not trying to impress him. "I came in yesterday afternoon. We said, hello, to each other and, I guess he decided we were going to be friends. In fact, I know him just about as long as I know you. My name's John Dekker. By the way, what's yours?"

"Carl, Carl Powers, but my friends call me Tex. You see, I'm from Texas."

"I never would have known that. I'm from a little town in Illinois. It's on Lake Michigan, it's called, Chicago."

"Yeah, I've heard of Chicago. That's where we send all our cows."

It never seems to fail; every time a country boy meets a city boy, they toy with each other. Tex was okay though, "a good ol' boy", as he would have put it. We were to be together for thirty days while going through orientation. It was just like boot camp; check your eyes, interviews with the bug doctor, draw your blood, do you go to church? What kind of work would you like to do while you're in Leavenworth? And then we were brought before a board of officers and the warden before being released into population. I was in the board room for approximately fifteen seconds.

Warden: "Dekker, you have ten years to serve. Where would you like to work?"

Me: "I would like to go to the farm, Sir."

Warden: "Dekker, we will do better than that. We'll send the farm to you. You are assigned to the vegetable room."

Tex and I both ended up in the dining hall. He served coffee, millions of gallons of coffee. I served bread, tons of bread. Tex and I were very unhappy with our new occupations. There didn't seem to be a future here, what kind of rehabilitation was this? After thirty days of this, I finally blew my top and tried to beat a guy to death with a loaf of bread. For this infraction of the rules, I was given seven days in the hole and ten days loss of good time. The hole was the pits. I loved the place. They had nothing but your health in mind. No cigarettes—bad for the lungs. Breakfast, a bowl of oatmeal and three slices of bread. Lunch, three slices of bread and a carrot. Supper, three slices of bread and a plate of gummy spaghetti, no sauce. Oh, yes, you could have all the water you wanted.

One thing I did appreciate about the hole, you were left alone and had nothing to do but sleep and think. For the first three days, I did nothing but fantasize of Bunny and the kids. I came to one conclusion: I was a jerk; I ruined their lives, I ruined my life and I wasn't worth two dead flies to any of us. It was then I made up my mind to escape. Come what may, hell or high water, I was going to give it a try. What's the difference if you get shot and killed going over the wall or die in a bed in a penitentiary. You end up in the same place anyway.

Well, one thing, the mess hall hadn't changed. I was put back to work passing out bread and managed to keep out of trouble I only had one thing on my mind now and I began looking for a way out. I told Tex I was planning to escape and he was all for it. He was doing fifteen years for bank robbery and that country boy and I thought just about alike. We had no plan yet and our connections in the joint were zero.

We knew nobody and nobody knew us. When you plan a jail break, you need tools, maybe a rope, a gun, things like that. They always come in handy. We had nothing. Another thing about a jail break, you just don't go around talking to anybody about it. That can get very touchy. It took me over a year to find the one man I trusted enough to enter this venture with us. I met him while attending school.

Harold Hendricks was six years older than me, had a fine education, and was teaching math in the prison school. I thought he had one hell of a sense of humor, but at the same time very profound. He had served a short time with the paratroopers, ending up with a dishonorable discharge and a German lugar he had picked up while on duty in Germany. Upon release from the service he tried, in vain, to find employment, but, with the dishonorable discharge hanging over his head, it was almost impossible. Finally, he gave up looking for work and put the lugar to work. Convicted of three bank robberies, he was sent to Leavenworth with three, ten-year sentences, running wild, thirty years total. I decided Hendricks was our man.

After several conversations, while in school and while walking the yard, I finally broached the subject in a joking way.

"Harold, do you think you'd need a parachute if you jumped off that wall?"

He looked at the wall. It was at least thirty feet high. "Na, I'd jump that without a chute. Probably break a leg, but I'd jump it to get out of here."

Then, not joking, "How would you like to try it with me?"

"I thought you'd never ask," he laughed. "When do we go?"

After much manipulating, we arranged to get a bar spreader made in the machine shop. How this was made and what it was made of, I will not say. But when the authorities found it, they had their experts look at it for their opinion. The experts said it would not only have spread the bars, it would have spread the eye-beams in the cell house.

Unfortunately, Tex, Harold and I were seen on a test run and one of our fellow inmates blew the whistle on us. Tex and I were shipped to Alcatraz the following month; Harold was held for trial because they found the bar spreader in his cell.

*Chapter 17*

## "Twelve Acres Of Hell"

It just wasn't fair. They showed no compassion at all, none. Was it that they just didn't care? It was a clear, star-studded night, not a cloud in the sky and only a slight mist over the bay. Why then, did they make us sit on long, hard benches in the hole of the boat? And the son-of-a-bitch that built the boat, he had no imagination, at all. The dummy forgot to put windows in it. No consideration at all. We glided across the water to the beat of powerful engines, and within ten minutes, we were at the dock of Alcatraz. As we unloaded, chains rattling, I gazed at our surroundings: thirty feet ahead of us was a yellow bus, similar to a school bus. Leading to the bus was a pathway, on each side of the pathway, to your right and left, were guards, dressed in gray with billy-clubs in their hands. I guess they were there to protect us. Well, we were well protected all right, because there were at least fifty of Uncle Sam's finest watching us closely.

Our leg irons clanking, we were loaded onto the bus and taken up a winding hill. From the windows of the bus, we had a great view of the Golden Gate Bridge off to our right. It was strange being able to look out of a window that didn't have mud all over it. Our sight-seeing tour was short-lived, and shortly thereafter, we were led into a room in the main building. It was in the basement and contained row upon row of shower heads. I figured it our right away, we were in the shower room.

Again, we were ordered to sit down on long, hard benches. Walking down each line of men, two officers began to take off our cuffs and leg irons. These, they threw into a box the size of an orange crate. We all felt one hundred pounds lighter and began to rub our sore wrists and ankles. We were then ordered to remove our coveralls, given a body search, and told to take a shower. Ten minutes later, we were on the long, hard benches again. I began to wonder, did we sleep on long, hard benches, too?

They timed it just right. Each of us sat there naked, shivering for about ten minutes before they brought us our prison clothes. Pants and shirt were blue—the shirt denim, the pants, I thought at the time, were made of canvas, but after a wash or two, they became very comfortable and warm.

Shortly after we got dressed, a runt in civilian clothes, escorted by two guards, walked into the room. He stood erect in front of us, his body guards at his side. His eyes swept the benches quickly, his head nodding slowly. He was thinking.

"Men," he cleared his throat. "I am captain of the guard, Williams. The inmates, here on Alcatraz, call me 'Humphrey Bogart' behind my back. Be that as it may, I call them a lot worse than that at times. My duties here, on Alcatraz, are to keep you people here until you are either released from your sentence or you die. You were sent to Alcatraz because the country clubs back on the mainland could not control you. We, here on Alcatraz, will control you! And a great deal depends on you. If you follow the rules, you will be treated fairly. If you do not follow the rules, you will be treated accordingly. Am I understood?"

He, again, ran his eyes up and down the benches. Satisfied he got his message across, he turned to leave, when a voice from a back bench said:

"He ain't no Humphrey Bogart. The dude ain't even got a rain coat."

Captain Williams' eyes shot cross the men sitting on the benches. "I've got you, though," he snarled.

There, you see, always some wise guy in the crowd. Now Captain Williams was going to be mad at us. I could tell, because he turned on his heel sharply and marched up the stairs in a huff.

I'm not the kind of guy that will let first appearances sway me, but I came to the conclusion after our first meeting with the captain. This man definitely had an acute case of meanness.

In twos, we were led up the stairs and walked directly to the center of the cell house. To our back was the mess hall, lights out and closed for the night. There went my hope for a snack before bedtime. In front of us was the main cell house. Two tiers of cells on each side of what the cons called Broadway. Each tier had approximately one hundred cells on it. The right bank of cells were empty, the left bank was where the black inmates celled. The right bank was kept empty except when a transfer of new men arrived on the island. There were four blocks of cells in Alcatraz; A block, B block, C block, and D block (the hole). Alcatraz could accommodate at least eight hundred prisoners and not be over crowded, but Uncle Sam could not find that many bad men to punish, or he figured eight hundred cons like us would surely blow up the island.

They marched us single file down Broadway until each man stood in front of a cell. Another guard yelled, "All clear!" And the cell door slammed shut behind us. The cell was decorated in Alcatraz decor: a bed, mattress, pillow and two blankets. They forgot to put a toilet seat on my toilet and the wash basin leaked. Other than that, it wasn't fit for a pig. It was cozy, though, I'd say eight feet long and four feet wide. I'll bet you could pee from the front of the cell and hit the toilet in the back.

Two minutes after we entered our cells, one of the guards came around and counted us. While standing there, I recognized a black fellow I had played baseball with in Leavenworth. He waved to me and said in a cheerful voice, "Welcome ta Alcatraz, figured you'd be along soon, John."

"Hey, Moose, how you doing, buddie? What's happening? When did you get out here?"

Moose showed all his teeth in a grin. This man was the most athletic person I have ever met. While in Leavenworth, he played all the sports, football, baseball, track and weightlifting, and he excelled in all of them. He was built like a tank, low to the ground and powerful. Had he taken up sports while in the free world, he no doubt would have ended up on the front page of the *Sporting News*. Instead, he had ended up on the ten most-wanted men list and received a thirty-year sentence for kidnapping a drug tsar in St. Louis, Mo.

"Got out here on da last shipment, John. They didn't tell me why they sent me here, they just done it. I think it was because the guy I snatched ended up in Leavenworth, too. And with me and him there together, one of us was sure gunna kill the other, so they shipped ol' Moose out here."

"Moose, have you got any candy or something? I'm hungry as hell."

"John, there ain't no commissary on da rock."

"How about bringing stuff in from the mess hall?"

"Yeah, dat's what I do, but tonight we had beef stew and dat's kinda hard to bring back to the cell. Know what I mean?"

"Later, Moose. I'm going to lay down and starve to death."

"You can't do dat, John. It's against da rules."

I pulled the chain and the over-hanging light went out. I took off my clothes, looked for a place to hang them and then let them drop to the floor. What a joint. I felt a chill in the air and got under my blanket, folded my hands under my head and prepared to sleep without the restrictions of the hand cuffs and leg irons. I was just entering the land of nod when I heard it.

"Get this frigging guy out of here . . . . ! Holy Christ! Get him out! I can't stand it!"

Suddenly the cells became silent, everyone stopped talking at once. And then it came out of the silence again, like a bull, snorting at the bull fights. Kenny Frazer was asleep. But nobody else would sleep that night.

*Chapter 18*

## "Everybody Loves Everybody"

Sir William Osler once said: "There's only one way to treat the common cold—with contempt."

It is my firm, undaunted opinion, that Warden Edwin Swope had the same idea about convicts. He was our glorious leader when I arrived on the rock. He was a man hated by both inmates and guards alike. He was a short man, perhaps one hundred thirty pounds, with the ego of a Napoleon and the guts of a wimp. Swope served as warden from 1948 until 1955. He retired to New Mexico, and while riding a horse was thrown and died from a ruptured spleen. When we heard about it, all of us cons wanted to pitch in money to send to New Mexico. We all wanted to buy a new blanket for the horse.

I think there was one guard that actually liked Swope, we called him, "Floppy Ears." I once had a run-in with him, when I took an orange back to the cell with me from the mess hall. He followed me back to the cell, wrote me up and then demanded the orange. The cell door was open, so I let it fly and it hit him right in the forehead. I felt bad about that, I was not aiming for his head. The next day I was brought before the disciplinary board. I feared the worst, at least seven days in the hole, but to my surprise, I was only restricted from two movies. My only conclusion, at that time, was that Associate Warden Latimer did not care for "Floppy Ears" either. I think it was because "Floppy Ears" was one of Swope's *rats,** or he didn't want to see a nice kid like me locked up in the hole for seven days.

* *Rat: An informer.*

Broadway was to be our home for the next week. In the meantime, we were given the bible (rule book) to study. This great piece of literature was promptly thrown on the shelf and forgotten. We were issued tooth paste, shaving soap, tooth brush and a towel. We were allowed one package of cigarettes every other day, compliments of Uncle Sam, and all the roll-your-owns you wanted.

During the week, we were taken out in groups of three or four and put to work dusting the bars, sweeping the floors and painting cells. It was all menial work, but work was considered a privilege and it sure felt good getting out of those cells. It also gave the guards an opportunity to study you and to know if you were a trouble maker or not. It took me three weeks to get a decent job in the prison industries. Most of the other fellows were put to work after a week on Broadway; some on the yard gang, others in the kitchen or cell house work. In a way I was lucky. I stayed on Broadway two extra weeks because old "You're in trouble now" reported me for telling him to go screw himself while we were on the choo-choo train. My punishment was to be two extra weeks on fish row, and fortunately, when my time was up, there was an opening in the industries and I was assigned a job. The industry job paid about a dollar a day and five days extra good time a month. The dollar I saved, the good time I cherished, it cut my time right in half. Had I started out getting industry good time the day I entered the penitentiary, I would have cut my ten-year sentence into a five year sentence. Why didn't somebody tell me that?

Each day was repeated the same way, up at 6:30 in the morning, wash up and clean the cell, and stand for count. We were allowed to have breakfast after the count cleared. Sometimes the little gray moneys got the count screwed up and we'd have to do it over again, but this only happened about fifteen times a week. I think they used a Chinese calculator.

After breakfast it was back to the cells for another count, get out hats and coats and off to work. We were marched down to the yard and stood on a line that indicated where we worked. We were then counted again (can you believe it?). After count we were taken down to our work area. As soon as we went to work, there was another count. Something told me that they didn't trust us. At 11:30 we would leave the work area and return to our cells for the noon meal. While going through the yard on the way to our cells, guards would suddenly grab a prisoner out of line and search him. They would do this at random and you didn't know if you were going to be next or not. Before we entered the cell house, we had to walk through an electronic walkway (snitch box). If we had any metal on us, the box would go off like a slot-machine. When the noon meal was completed, we had sick call, and then it was back to work. We'd go through the same procedure; count in the yard and then down to work. At 4:30, we would leave the industries, go through the search and the snitch box and finally to our humble cells.

Another count and we were off to supper. We'd be back in our cells about 5:30, stand yet another count and then be left alone until morning. At 9:30 the lights would go out and we left Alcatraz by escaping into sleep.

This routine was followed five days a week. The only time you did not work was when there was a heavy fog, you were sick, or was in the hole. We, in industry, looked forward to the weekends. It was a time to relax. On the weekends, we hit the yard, played baseball (on concrete), played cards, walked the yard or played handball for cigarettes. Every other weekend, we had a movie. You were free to go to church if you felt like it, and surprisingly, church was usually filled to capacity. Most of us didn't believe in the law, but we believed in the Man upstairs.

When you are caged up in a four-by-eight cell for twelve hours a day, seven days a week, you become an animal, ready to jump at the first person that gives you any problems. We all knew this, therefore, we watched what we said, and as a rule, we all got along pretty good. Today in the penitentiary, there are groups of men that form small gangs. On Alcatraz, we were one big gang. There was no pretense about it, we had

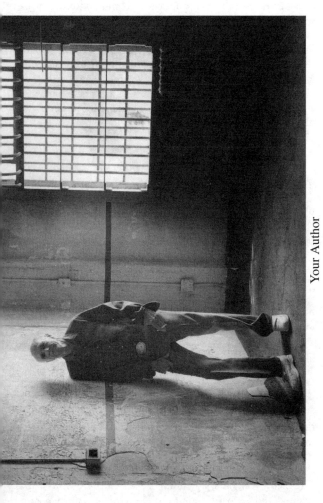

Your Author
Went back to the old homestead

only one enemy, the establishment . . . I must admit, they always won the battle, but they did not win the war.

On my very first weekend in the yard, I was walking with Tex and Moose when I heard a commotion behind us. We turned quickly and I witnessed my first murder on Alcatraz. Moose grabbed me by the arm, spun me around and said, "Keep walking, John. Dat man's dead, ya can't help him. Just act like ya didn't see nuttin', or you'll end up in court as a witness. Come on, just cool it."

"What the hell was that all about?" I asked.

"Da guy dat got killed, was a punk. Da guy what killed him was in love wit him." Moose said it like it was a lover's quarrel.

"He loved him?" I wondered what he would have done if he hated him.

They carried the dead man up the stairs to the cell house on a stretcher. The other man walked quietly up the stairs, two guards in front of him and two guards behind him. When he got to the top of the steps, he turned, waved at the men in the yard and walked into the cell house. I never saw the man again, he committed suicide while in the treatment unit (the hole). Where he got the razor blade I don't know. But I do know this, his war was over.

That was on a Saturday. I made up my mind to attend church on Sunday.

The one thing I can't complain about while in Alcatraz, was the food. Our meals were as good as the military and many of the officers ate the same food we did. You could just about bet on what you would be eating from one week until the next. On holidays, you could usually expect a steak, mashed potatoes, gravy, a vegetable and pie. Thanksgiving was turkey day. Pie or cake was often served in the evening, sometimes ice cream.

Once a year, on a Jewish holiday, an inmate, Abby Chapman, would get permission from the warden to make potato pancakes for the prison population. Abby was his nickname. A jolly fella, but most untidy. He never buttoned his fly or combed his bushy hair. But on the one day he would prepare the potato pancakes, you would have thought he was going to a meeting with the Queen of England. His pants were pressed, and his hair was slicked down on each side. When he walked into the mess hall, he walked with his shoulders squared, and had a beaming smile across his face. One and all, the inmates would applaud his entrance. Abby was a pleasant, quiet man. Everyone liked him. He was also a hit-man for Murder, Inc.

And then there was Johnny Revense, a New Jersey bank robber. A real cock-of-the-walk Italian. He had been on the same shipment to Alcatraz as I, and from what I remember, the guy never shut up. He was a short man, perhaps 110 pounds, tops. Johnny, like most Italians, loved his spaghetti. Once a week we had spaghetti and Johnny was allowed to enter the mess hall fifteen minutes before the rest of the men. I think it was the only time he kept his mouth shut. The plates we received our meals on had five compartments. Johnny would load the plate until the spaghetti hung over the sides in ringlets. He would then saturate the spaghetti with sauce. It took both of his hands to take the plate back to his table. The strange thing about it, the guy never put on a pound.

*Chapter 19*

## "Nobody Walks On Water"

Harold arrived on Alcatraz on the next shipment and we got together in the yard the following weekend. He seemed thinner, his face was drawn and the smile was gone. We must have walked up and down the yard thirty times before he spoke.

"They gave me another five spot, John. Now I find out I've got a detainer from Michigan. Armed robbery. Hell man, I'll never see the streets again."

"Yeah, the way it looks, you'll be seeing a lot of water for a while, unless . . ."

"Unless what?"

"Unless you can walk on water," his face showed disappointment. "I'm just kidding." I said, and he smiled for the first time that day.

"What have you got in mind, John?"

"It's not what you think, buddie. I'm not going to bust out of this joint for nothing. But there's a way out for you." I pointed to the steps. "Let's take a breather, I want you to meet somebody."

I had spotted Courtney Taylor while Harold and I had been walking. As soon as Harold had mentioned the detainer he had from Michigan, my mind had begun to click. Courtney and I had a running chess game going, and I usually played with him in the afternoon. This man was not the run-of-the-mill con. He was in his late sixties, hair of grey and had sharp blue eyes. He was only about five foot three, but he stood tall in my eyes. I could never beat him at chess, he would spot me the queen and still put me down. He was a master at chess, and he was a wizard at law, considered the best writ man in the prison system.

I introduced Harold to Courtney and told Harold to explain his case to him. I then went down to the handball court and made a fool out of myself. These guys had been playing for years and drove me clean across the yard every time they hit the ball. I soon tired of this and began to walk in the yard again. When I arrived at the end of the yard, I stopped and watched the men playing cards. There was a grey-hair fella sitting alone at a table, I nodded to him and said, "Hello."

He smiled back at me and pointed to the table. "You ever play the game of dominoes, Sonny?"

"A little."

"Well, sit down here then. We have time for one game before we go to chow. Maybe you can show me a little about the game."

I showed him, all right. In that half hour before chow, he beat me out of five packs of cigarettes. I admired the man, he had class written all over him. He spoke softly and his blue eyes sparkled when he talked. He was about sixty, still had all his hair and wore it in a crew-cut. His name was Alvin Karpis. His nickname was "Creepy" but there was nothing creepy about this man. To me, he was a gentleman. He never, at any time, tried to impress me or brag about his crimes. It was only through one of my friends that I discovered who the man really was. It was hard to believe that this man, across the domino table from me, was who they said he was.

Alvin Karpis was, at one time, a Public Enemy No. l. In the history of the United States, there have been only four Public Enemies No. l: John Dillinger, killed in Chicago; Baby Face Nelson, killed; Pretty Boy Floyd, killed. Alvin Karpis was the only man that did not go down in a hail of gun fire. His fate had been worse, he served 33 years in prison, most of it on Alcatraz.

Karpis was convicted of kidnapping William Hamm, the brewery king. While on the run, he knew his time was growing short, so he tried to have his fingerprints removed and plastic surgery done on his face.

J. Edgar Hoover made a claim that he had captured Alvin Karpis, almost single handedly, in New Orleans. This is myth. There are two versions to this story. Alvin Karpis, himself, had admitted the F.B.I.. did a top-rate job in tracing him to New Orleans through the marked bills he had received on the kidnapping of a bank president in Minnesota. But, J. Edgar Hoover was smoking a cigar in his car three blocks away when the arrest was made. I tend to believe Alvin Karpis. Until the day J. Edgar Hoover died, Alvin Karpis swore to this and I believed him. Alvin Karpis died in 1979, a free man.

Clarence Carnes was a good friend of mine. He was the youngest man to be sent to Alcatraz, entering the prison when he was eighteen. He was an Indian kid from Oklahoma, full-blooded Choctaw. One night, full of fire water, Carnes, with another kid, went out and killed a paleface during a robbery. He received a life sentence in the Oklahoma State Penitentiary and soon made his escape. Shortly after that, he was caught while driving a car across the state line (a Federal rap) that was enough to get him sent to THE ROCK. Most of his time on Alcatraz he spent in the hole because of his attempted escape in the big one of 1946. In that escape, three cons were killed, sixteen guards were wounded and one guard was killed. Clarence Carnes also died a free man.

The oldest man ever admitted to Alcatraz was James Alex Carter, the date was December 9th, 1935. He must have been one real bad dude at the age of seventy-two. Either that, or they wanted him to play Santa Claus. Why the U. S. Department of Justice would send a seventy-two-year-old man to Alcatraz is something I'll never be able to figure out. This is something I would not be proud of. Perhaps that's why it has never been mentioned before.

J.B.             Your Author             Willie
                Planning a heist!

*Chapter 20*

# "Na, They Didn't Believe Me"

We were going into Christmas week when Harold was notified by the Michigan authorities that they were going to honor his detainer on the armed robbery charge, and he would be brought to trial within ninety days. Courtney Taylor had won another battle in the courts of our land. He had orchestrated a writ for Harold, that would have been upheld in the Supreme Court of Michigan, and the lower court had no alternative, but to grant Harold's petition. Had Harold hired a lawyer from the street, it would have cost him several thousand dollars to prepare his case. Courtney, after hundreds of hours of research and hand written briefs, had charged Harold the grand total of ten tins of snuff, equivalent to about ten dollars in a street tobacco shop.

Harold was picked up by the Michigan authorities in late February, 1954, and transferred by train. Somewhere, between Alcatraz and the Wayne County Jail, Detroit, Michigan, Harold managed to escape. They could never figure out how he had managed to get out of his hand cuffs and make his break to freedom. I think it was because Harold and I had made a hand cuff key out of the ink cylinder from a ballpoint pen before he departed from Alcatraz.

The F.B.I.. had an interview with me concerning Harold's escape. I was honest with them. I told them I knew nothing about it. Somehow, I feel they did not believe me.

Harold was later caught in the midwest, and was transferred from the county jail in that particular town, to a hospital for the insane. He would be sixty-five now, and is either dead or on the run. One thing I do know, Harold was never returned to Alcatraz.

Dudley Owens, Photographer
Checking out escape route of the Morris Crew

Alcatraz usually had a population of around two hundred and fifty inmates. Each year, approximately fifty new men would be admitted to the institution, fifty old timers would be shipped back to the country clubs on the mainland. They were mostly short timers, ready to be discharged or turned over to another jurisdiction for trial. This was what they call, doing time on the installment plan. You did five, ten or even twenty-five years on the rock. That wasn't good enough for them, they wanted more, they wanted their ounce of flesh, too....

*Chapter 21*

---

## *"You Win Some, You Lose Some"*

---

While on Alcatraz, I had many discussions with the old-timers, as we walked the yard. They unfolded many stories of their youth, and their adventures in crime. One such story told to me was about Al Capone. It was so far out of line that I just dismissed it from my mind.

Big Al Capone, while on Alcatraz, was slowly dying from syphilis of the brain. Hardly anybody paid any attention to him or his far-out stories. John Paul Chase, bank robber, and a good friend of Baby Face Nelson, was one of the few people that did listen to Al and his tall tales. John Paul was doing life for the killing of an F.B.I.. agent while in the company of Baby Face Nelson. He, too, had a few tales he could tell.

It seems, Al Capone, while in power, had gathered up a great deal of loot, while in the business of running Chicago's whore houses, drugs and bootlegging. According to Al, his money was stashed all over the country. He did not tell John Paul exactly where he had this wealth hidden, but he did say it was someplace in northern Nevada, in an old silver mine.

Just recently, a fabulous treasure was found in an old silver mine near Carson City, Nevada. There was over thirty million in gold, silver bars, and a chest full of precious jewels. Was this the hidden hoard of Al Capone?

Alcatraz, in the beginning, 1934, was opened primarily for housing the gangsters of that era. The Dillingers, the Nelsons and the Floyds, but the grim reaper managed to get them first. The FBI, along with the Department of Justice, fooled the public into thinking this was still the case, when it really wasn't. There were many men sent to Alcatraz that were undeserving of that fate. True, they should have been in prison, but Alcatraz? No.

Rafael Miranda was an example of this deception. He belonged on Alcatraz about as much as Bugs Bunny did. His crime was strictly political, a foolish endeavor, on his part, to gain independence for Puerto Rico. Rafael was a quiet, polite, religious gentleman. His eyes were a deep black, and had a calming effect.

Rafael was convicted, along with two of his countrymen, while trying to blow up the Hall of Congress with hand grenades. His picture appeared in *Life* and *Newsweek*. He was portrayed as a killer of babies and old ladies. With such adverse publicity going against him, he was considered a threat to society, and a candidate for Alcatraz. His crime was violent and he deserved what he got, but not Alcatraz.

While on Alcatraz, I received two visits (not counting the FBI), my mother and dad on one occasion; my brother, Bill, and his wife on the other. Each visit was tearful and very depressing. These good people had traveled half way across the country, just to look through a glass window and talk to their son over a telephone. It was degrading to the inmates, and a direct insult to their loved ones. When they reached the island, the visitors were searched, and run through a snitch box. We, the inmates, were strip-searched before and after the visit. All this searching, this big deal security, just to look through a window, and talk over a telephone.

There was not too much visiting on Alcatraz, because 95% of the inmates had asked their loved ones not to come back. The super prison was bush league, when it came to human feelings.

It was belittling things, such as visits, that drove some inmates to insane deeds. I think the government stayed up to all hours of the night, devising ways to break down the inmates' resistance. To play with their minds, this was a ploy the officials used at every opportunity. Anything and everything could, and did, happen, because of this relationship between

Could this be "The Ghost of Alcatraz?"

guards and inmates. Riots and attempted escapes were common, you can also throw in several suicides.

Alcatraz received its first prisoner on June 19th, 1934. The prisoner, who had this honor of being "number one" in the gangsters hall of fame, was Frank L. Bolt, age twenty-five, transferred from the U.S. Army Disciplinary Barracks, Fort Leavenworth, Kansas.

The last man to enter Alcatraz was Peter S. Scherk, age thirty-two.

From 1934 until March 21. 1963, fifteen hundred and fifty-seven men crossed San Francisco Bay to set foot on these twelve acres of hell. In that span, twenty-eight years, there were fourteen escape attempts. The establishment called them escape attempts. We inmates, called them suicide attempts. You could call them nothing else. In these attempts of madness, thirteen men died; seven shot to death, and six by drowning. To me, those odds are worse than the lottery. You had the cold water to contend with (fifty-eight degrees) and a mile and an eighth swim to the mainland, against tides running five to ten miles an hour. That's after you beat the count, tied up at least one guard, and scaled a ten-foot wall covered with barbed wire.

Joseph Bowers, age forty, was the first man to make a break for freedom. It was April 27th 1936, at 11:00 a.m. He was shot like a sitting duck from off a cyclone fence and died on the rocks below. Bowers, according to the old-timers, was a dim-witted man with the brain of a child. He was a victim of the 'Policy': "Death to he who tries to escape." If he had a gun with him, or a speed boat waiting, you could call the killing justified, but he had neither. I'll let you be the judge . . . .

Escape fourteen was successful in a manner of speaking. At least one man, John Paul Scott, managed to swim to the mainland. He was found clinging to a rock, half frozen and exhausted. He had beaten the rock, but the cold waters of the bay had beaten him.

There were several inmates among us that could be considered low-profile, mystery men. These men caused very little

Whitey Thompson
Tough guy with a soft heart

trouble to the establishment, meaning average behavior; once or twice in the hole, two or three fights, maybe making a little brew once in a while, things of that nature. I, myself, was only thrown in the hole twice. Once, for fighting in the yard with a very good friend, J.B. It was one of those spur of the moment things and should never have happened. I take full responsibility for this and J.B. should never have been put in the hole. It was a short-lived battle that took six guards to break up. At the end of the fight, I had my finger in J.B.'s eye, just about ready to pluck it, when something stopped me. Whatever it was, I don't know, but I thank God for it now. J.B., in turn, had me in real trouble. We were both in deep trouble. Again, I say thanks, for, if either of us had completed our battle plan, J.B. would be wearing a patch today and I would be singing tenor in some choir.

No, the only time I really rebelled was the one time with "Floppy Ears," and I believe to this day that if the man had a gun, he would have shot me. Knowing "Floppy Ears," he would have pleaded self defense. After all, I had an orange.

Willy Thompson arrived on the rock in the summer of 1957. You could consider Willy a clone for one of the Three Stooges. He had that effect, because his dress was sloppy, his manner girlish and he seemed to be walking on his heels all the time. A real character. But Willy Thompson was a mental genius, his brains had brains. He owned and ran a multi-million dollar junk yard business on the west coast, and he had been convicted of buying tons of lead from the black market, lead contaminated with deadly uranium . . . Willy was a bad boy. He was given a nickname by the guys on Alcatraz. He was called: "Suit Case Sally." It had come over the grapevine that Thompson had tried to smuggle money into the prison when he first arrived. He had hidden the money in a tube containing several hundred dollars in his rectum, and during his body search it was found. Thus, the name, "Suit Case Sally."

Whitey died and Joe lived. Two good friends of mine. Whitey Hill was a good-natured farm boy from Indiana, convicted of a post office robbery. The post office happened to be in a small town drug store. He went to rob the drug store for drugs, but because there was a post office on the premises, the Feds moved in and gave Whitey a twenty-five year sentence, for a sixteen dollar robbery.

Joe Sanchez was a Mexican boy from New Mexico, and a very quiet individual, who managed to stay in trouble most of his life. First, stealing cars for a joy ride, and then turning to bank robbery. Joe was doing a twenty-five year jolt, with about six detainers waiting for him. Whitey and Joe were very good friends. Between them, they put in about ten miles apiece walking the yard every weekend. If Joe got into trouble and ended up in the hole, Whitey would go out and beat some stool pigeon senseless, just so he would be thrown in the hole to be with Joe. They were "rock partners." You fooled with Joe, you had to contend with Whitey, too.

We were served chili once a week on Alcatraz. This was a big night for Joe. He would load his plate up to the brim, and often go back for seconds. Being Mexican, he ate the chili like it was candy. It saved his life.

After supper, on a night we had chili, Joe and Whitey drank a concoction of home brew that they made in the industries. The next morning, Whitey was dead and Joe was blind. Whitey didn't eat chili; his belly was empty; that's what killed him. Joe, blind as a bat, is probably somewhere in New Mexico today, waving a cane, and selling apples. Knowing Joe, he's probably saying to himself, "Why did I eat all that chili?"

Nate Williams
Gentleman bandit, always said thank you and have a nice day

*Chapter 22*

## "One Is A Man, The Other Is A Dog"

While on Alcatraz, I was assured of a steady job. As long as I stayed out of trouble, I would be able to make a few dollars a month and gather up that ever lovin' good time. Nobody on the outside would work for the wage we received and only a mule would work as hard, but to us prisoners it was the only way we could get away from laying around all day in a cell and getting fat.

Ed Byrnes had more time in the tailor shop than anyone I knew, possibly twenty or twenty-five years. He was a powerfully built man, with large brown eyes, behind glasses that looked like they had been made from the bottom of a soda pop bottle. Without his glasses, Ed would need a seeing-eye dog. He was a shy man, and as long as I was in the tailor shop (four years), I never heard him raise his voice.

Ed was a great sports fan, always talking baseball, boxing and football. 'Say Hey' Willy Mays was his hero, and Rocky Marciano was the greatest fighter that ever lived. On occasion, a group of celebrities would stop for a tour of Alcatraz. When this happened, ol' Ed would be in his glory. Just like a kid, he would prance around the tailor shop squinting through his thick glasses.

Because of the work he did, and partly because he was so shy, Ed would never approach a celebrity and ask for an autograph. Ed was really a pussy cat, so I did the job for him. If I blew my assignment, so what. I liked Ed Byrnes and so did every man in the tailor shop.

In all, I must have got ten autographs for Ed through the years. He never offered me anything for them. He just nodded his head and said, "Thanks, Deck."

Ed Byrnes died a few years ago. And I will remember him the rest of my life. He was a gentle, considerate man, and the best prison guard I ever knew.

I guess Alcatraz could not have been that bad, not according to the record anyway. Thirty-one inmates managed to be admitted twice; of these inmates, four were friends of mine. The fifth man was Floyd G. Mann. (We called him Dog.) It seems odd that a man can't have at least one friend in this world, but Dog had that curse, and he lived a miserable existence, in and out of prison.

Dog was ugly in every sense of the word; his face was pock-marked, his teeth were yellow and broken off from the many fights he'd been in, and he had an obnoxious personality, to boot. He was a stool-pigeon and would steal his grandma's pacemaker, if he could.

One afternoon, in the summer of 1955, while everybody was out walking the yard, Dog Mann met his Waterloo. Simcox (A real loony tune, himself) walked up to Dog, grabbed him around the throat, and stabbed him three times in the chest and two times in the face. Dog's tongue was cut in half and his chest was a mass of blood. They rushed him to the prison hospital emergency room, where he laid half dead, until a crew of top notch doctors from the San Francisco Marine Hospital arrived by boat.

According to the prison grapevine, Dog's life was saved only because a St. Bernard dog on the island gave him a blood transfusion. Only on Alcatraz would a joke like that be funny.

Simcox, in 1956, killed his best friend in the shower room. He was brought to trial and found not guilty by reason of insanity. That was one jury that knew what they were talking about. Simcox was a maniac, and a born killer.

Dog also died in 1956.

*Chapter 23*

## *"Evicted!"*

May 14th, 1958. It's the big day for me. After four years and eleven months on the rock, I am finally released. Uncle Sam could no longer hold me. By law, he must turn me loose into society. He may not want to, but he had no choice. I've did my time.

It was a beautiful day, picture perfect, not a cloud in the sky. But it didn't matter to me, there could have been a tornado out on San Francisco Bay, and I couldn't have been happier. The prison boat took about ten minutes to reach the dock on the mainland. I was accompanied by the prison clerk and we just talked about things in general.

"You know, John, you are only the second man ever to be directly released from Alcatraz," the clerk said. "You're making history."

I didn't answer him.

He continued again, trying to be friendly. "What's your plans, John. What do you intend doing, now that you're a free man?"

I had to think about that. I had no trade to fall back on. While I had been on Alcatraz, I was taught to do time, and that was all.

"I was thinking about getting into the car business," I answered.

"Now that's a good idea, John. There will always be cars around," his voice was sincere, "and a man can make a good living if he knows what he's doing."

"I know what I'm doing."

When we arrived at the dock, he shook my hand, gave me my train ticket, and bid me good luck.

As I was turning to leave, he asked, "What kind of car business you going to get into, John? Fixing, buying and selling, what?"

I couldn't help grinning when the answer popped into my head.

"I was thinking about the armored car business. Good money in that, wouldn't ya say?"

I left him there with a blank look on his face.

"Just kidding," I said, or was I?

*THE BEGINNING*

# See the story of John Dekker and other Alcatraz ex-cons and guards in the award-winning documentary ALCATRAZ REUNION!

*"An unconventional reunion of epic proportions."*
-San Francisco Bay-Guardian Weekly Pick

What happens when America's most notorious prison hosts an 'alumni' reunion? Join the actual ex-inmates of Alcatraz as they return to the Rock for an unlikely reunion with their former cellhouse guards. Against the backdrop of this strange but true rendezvous, *Alcatraz Reunion* traces the history of America's most legendary penitentiary, and its mysterious transformation from fearsome prison to tourist mecca. *Directed by John Paget - USA - 77 minutes*

 Now available on DVD or digital download:
**www.AlcatrazReunion.com**